BRITAIN
FROM
ABoVE

BRITAIN
FROM
ABOVE

IAN HARRISON
FOREWORD BY ANDREW MARR

PAVILION

First published in the United Kingdom in 2008 by
Pavilion Books
10 Southcombe Street
London, W14 0RA

An imprint of Anova Books Company Ltd
© Pavilion 2008

Produced in association with Lion Television, 26 Paddenswick Road, London W6 0UB

The moral right of the author has been asserted.

Project Manager: Frank Hopkinson
Designer: Georgina Hewitt
Associate Publisher: Anna Cheifetz

ISBN 978-1-862058-34-7

A CIP catalogue record for this book is available from the British Library.

10 9 8 7 6 5 4 3 2 1

Reproduction by Rival Colour, United Kingdom
Printed and bound by SNP Leefung Printers Ltd, China

www.anovabooks.com

Previous page: Prickwillow, Cambridgeshire
This page: Seals on sandbanks off Great Yarmouth, Norfolk
Contents page: Millennium Wheel, London
Endpapers: Front - China clay lake near St Austell. Back - Tipis at Glastonbury

Dedicated to my mum, Mary Harrison, for providing the geography gene.

With special thanks to Frank Hopkinson and Polly Powell at Anova Books for their expert
guidance; to Rebecca Winch and Lucy van Beek at Lion TV for answering endless questions
and fulfilling countless requests, and to Jason Hawkes for his stunning aerial photographs.
Thanks also to my wife Caroline and daughters Megan and Edie for putting up with the stress
of a very tight schedule, and to everyone involved in the television production who was willing
to clarify points and answer questions. Last but not least, thanks to the following experts and
programme contributors for checking facts or/and giving permission to quote them: Garth
Earls, Paul Finch, Professor Bill Hillier, Dr Dougal Jerram, Stuart Ring, Sir Richard Rogers.

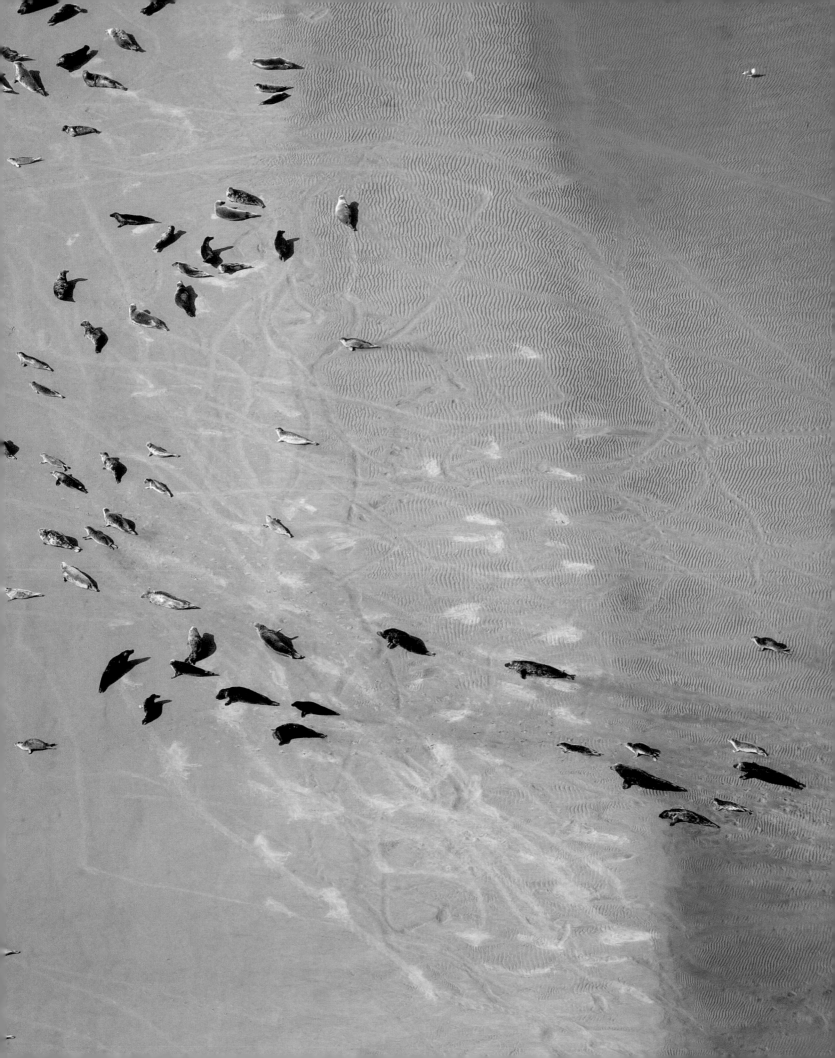

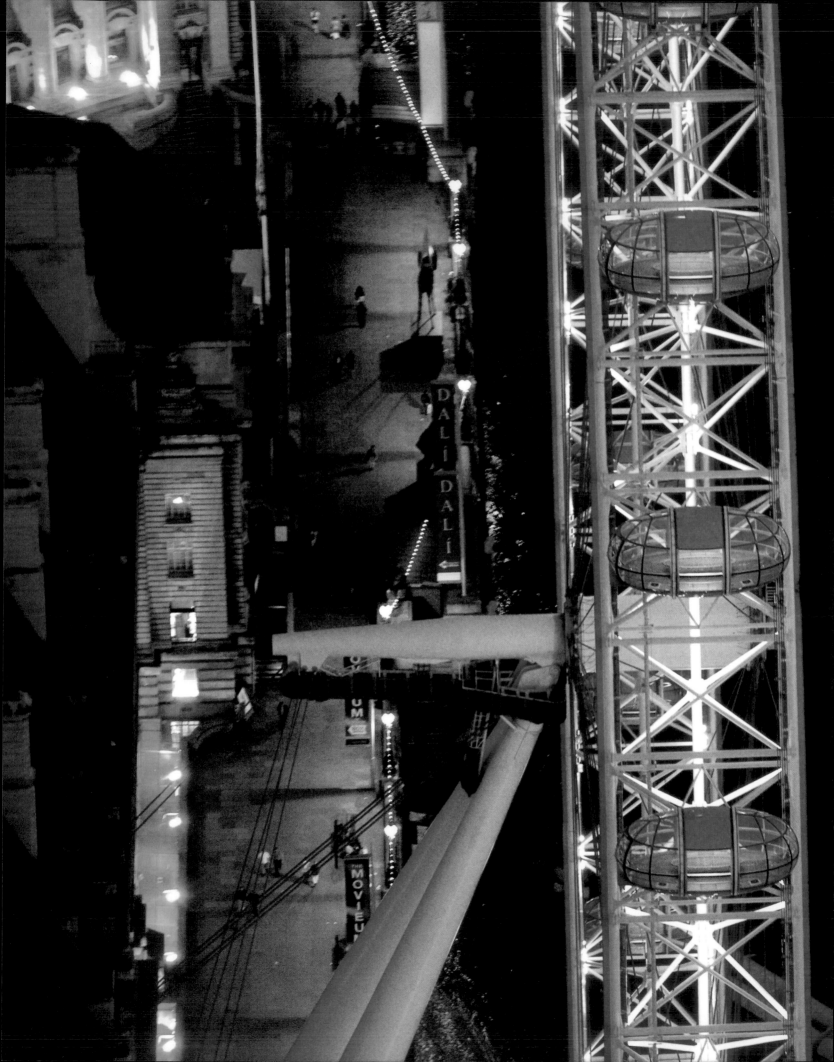

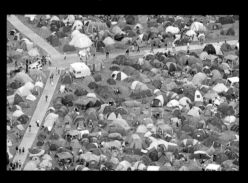

FOREWORD

Often the best ideas are the simple ones. Trying to discover what you can tell about Britain by hanging over it and looking down is about as simple as any television idea could be. It is one of those, 'nobody thought of that before?' ideas. Of course, most of us have a vague idea of what Britain looks like from above. We have flown on holiday, or on business, taking off from blandly impersonal airports, rising high through the clouds and glimpsing the undulations of green, brown and silvery cityscapes through gaps. Sometimes, passing low on takeoff or landing, we may even have seen our own streets and houses. Others of us have had trips in hot air balloons, or tried hang-gliding, or simply bought one of those aerial photographs of our area, or hovered over a laptop screen with Google Earth. In a sense, even using a map is trying to see Britain from above – a map, after all, is only a drawing of the country as it might be seen by a literal-minded, knowledgeable and English-speaking pigeon. So what can a project like this offer that these ordinary look-down moments do not?

The first thing is the sheer variety of perspectives. State-of-the-art helicopter mounted cameras that neither rock nor judder in high winds can pick out remarkable detail none of us would spot from a commercial flight. Lasers fired from aircraft can reveal hidden secrets under forest canopies. Microlite aircraft can take you down to a hawk's-eye view of rippling mountains, without the clutter of an ordinary plane. Cameras mounted on cranes can pick out and analyse the real movement of motorway traffic; careful, methodical aerial photography can reveal ancient archaeological sites and the true tale of dramatic coastal erosion. The 'toys' employed to make *Britain From Above* have been, I confess, huge fun. But they have (mostly) had a point as well.

Yet the real contribution brought to the project – more than a multi-channel television series, a large interactive website and this book too – comes from the expert eye. A wide range of historians, archaeologists, scientists, geologists, amateur sleuths, sportsmen, city planners, transport experts and others have willingly given their time and knowledge to unpick what the rest of us would certainly miss. Time and again, I have been taken aback by how much I simply did not see, however hard I looked. It might have been when standing on a Welsh hillside with a world-champion paraglider, and listening as he watched the apparently empty air below us, reading a small book of signs and hints about where the warm updrafts could be found. Or when stumbling through a Wiltshire forest to find that, under a thick layer of anonymous-looking bracken, nettles and thorns, there was an ancient temple hidden. Or again, when walking through the narrowest alleyways in the City of London with the man in charge of its planning, I found out that he had deliberately kept them out of reach of developers because of their pubs and coffee houses; for as he said, 'London is a trading city, and trade needs gossip.'

Though I have always thought of myself as relatively well educated, I had no idea about the complex relationship of geology to our lives; or just how man-made even some of the wildest-seeming areas, from the Fens to the Brecon Beacons, really are. I had no idea of the vastness of some of the armament dumps in the middle of England, nor why poorer, working class areas of cities are generally sited to their east. I did not know why it is so hard to travel by train across the country, compared to

journeying from north to south. Britain is a land full of local knowledge, full of world-class technical and academic expertise – full, in short, of clever people with something to share. It was a treat to hear them and I hope some of that sluices through these pages and the programmes themselves.

Is there a conclusion to be gleaned? After months of talking, looking and travelling, it is impossible not to be impressed anew by the roiling, bubbling and borderline-chaotic energy of the country. Britain is a most unnatural place. Over the centuries, our landscapes have been scribbled over, rewritten, rubbed out and replaced again and again. Tracks, ancient paths, railway lines and roads writhe everywhere, jostling the power lines, the sewage pipes and the invisible but increasingly busy flight-paths. There are wild corners and seemingly untouched national verges, but they are often an illusion. Compared to most countries, Britain has almost always been busy with human population; compared to most countries now, she is very busy, indeed crowded. The trains, roads, housing, hospitals and schools are crammed. A whole country seems at times to be creaking at the edges. In everyday life, most of us feel mildly outraged when something fails to work – when a train is cancelled, or our car is brought to a standstill on a motorway, or there are no apples in the supermarket. Yet from the 'above' perspective what is truly remarkable is that we function so relatively well – that so little goes wrong, so relatively rarely.

Should we therefore praise the politicians and the public services? Sometimes, no doubt, though the lack of long-term thinking and planning in recent decades, compared to the big thinking of Victorians and Edwardians, is a constant disappointment. There are many skilled, dedicated, practical-minded people keeping the country working, all around us, and too often taken for granted. But I came away thinking that the biggest reason for the continued functioning of this vast, intricate living system that is Britain – an ecology as complex in its way as any rainforest – was simply the tolerance, good humour and mutual respect of the people themselves. We have long traditions of being crowded, of getting along, of avoiding chaos, of maintaining historic links and – frankly – of bodging and dodging. Britain from above is a glorious sight. But to understand quite why it works, you have to land again, return to earth and rub shoulders with the sixty-something million busy dots below.

Andrew Marr

INTRODUCTION

BELOW: *Britain From Above* presenter Andrew Marr delivering a piece to camera from the roof of Manchester's tallest building, the 169-metre Beetham Tower.
RIGHT: A skateboard park in Stoke-on-Trent, Staffordshire.

The brief for the television series *Britain From Above* was to portray the nation as it has never been seen before. From the air, the UK is revealed as a national machine, its myriad interconnections always on; a machine whose crowded road and rail networks move 48 million people from place to place every working day, whose hidden infrastructures deliver all our daily needs and wants and take away our waste, and whose appearance is constantly being reshaped by humans and by the forces of nature.

This is not a conventional book of aerial photographs – there are no grand shots of Britain's castles, cathedrals or stately homes, no stunning vistas of our magnificent coastline and most famous tourist attractions; rather, it is packed with the unusual, the industrial, the hidden and the quirky – sewage works, power stations, motorway junctions and airports; coastal erosion, theme parks, oil refineries and open cast mines. As well as a new perspective on things we already know from ground level, the view from above reveals some surprising and less well known features of the United Kingdom – an ancient settlement hidden beneath an English forest, Northern Irish gold reserves, the world's tallest rotating tower in Scotland and how they held back the tide in Wales.

Television is a medium of moving images, jump cuts, multiple narratives and, in the case of *Britain From Above*, a witty presenter speaking directly to the viewer. Inevitably, then, the structure of this book-of-the-series differs from the programmes upon which it is based. But the essence of the book is the same as the series – a unique, compelling and

often surprising journey through the story of Britain, starting 600 million years ago when our landmass lay south of the equator and ending in 2012 with a preview of the London Olympic Park.

As well as being packed with stunning new aerial images by Britain's pre-eminent aerial photographer, Jason Hawkes, the book captures the drama and surprises of the series thanks to the inclusion of dozens of images from the programmes. These images include archive photographs, architects' drawings, computer-generated images, LiDAR and PSInSar™ images, and screen grabs like the one to the left , which is taken directly from the footage shot for the programme. And the book has some distinct advantages over the series – readers have the leisure to pore over images in detail, to play spot-the-difference with the 'then and now' images in the *Rewinds* chapter, and to marvel at the array of fascinating statistics unearthed by *Britain From Above* – that the nation has 10,295 miles of railway and 241,104 miles of roads; 5,000 miles of electric cables in the National Grid and 485,790 miles of water and sewage pipes; that we landfill more than 16.9 million tons of rubbish every year, and that Britons make more than eighty-seven cash machine withdrawals every second.

Translating over six hours of television into 208 pages while the programmes were still being made entailed constantly changing the content of the book to make it as faithful to the series as possible but despite those efforts there are elements of the series that do not appear

in the book and vice versa. The text is based on shooting scripts and transcripts of interviews with the experts who appear in the programmes, but they have been rearranged in a way that makes most sense on the page. *The rocks beneath our feet* tells the story of the British Isles themselves – the very ground we walk on – but it is no geology lesson: here is the story of why Ben Nevis is no longer as tall as Everest, why Vera Lynn is no naturalist, and why large areas of the British landscape are rising up into the air. *Shaping the land* examines how Britons have shaped the landscape for agriculture, industry and leisure, and *Untamed Britain* explores our weather, but they are not geography or meteorology lessons: here are stories of squirrels travelling the length of the UK through the treetops without touching the ground; farmers using satellites to tend their fields; a parachutist being trapped in a thundercloud, and the widespread destruction caused by Britain's worst droughts, floods and storms.

Hidden Britain provides a rare glimpse of places which most people can only ever see from the air because they are out of bounds to the public, such as Ministry of Defence munitions dumps, listening posts and combat training villages. *London skyline* takes a detailed look at the grand plans for the UK's capital – what might have been and what actually came to be, including insights from one of Britain's greatest architects, Sir Richard Rogers. In conjunction with the *Britain From Above* website www.bbc.co.uk.britainfromabove, the *Rewinds* chapter is packed with 'then and now' aerial shots revealing just how much Britain has changed since the Second World War, and provides a fascinating series of spot-the-difference competitions taking in everything from the Watford Gap service station on the M1, via steelworks, riverscapes, shopping centres and shipyards, to a former Butlins holiday camp in Ayr.

The great migration and *Demand and supply* look at the bold and compelling concept of Britain as a complex national machine, often on the brink of chaos but usually achieving what is required through a series of interconnected networks. *The great migration* concentrates on the transport networks that keep people moving in their millions every day, explaining why it is easy to travel up and down the country but much harder to travel across it, why commuters are called commuters, and why motorway traffic often grinds to a halt for no discernible reason. *Demand and supply* uncovers the less obvious networks: the hidden infrastructures of pipelines and cables that bring us gas, electricity, oil and water; and the intricacies of the 'just in time' delivery process that goes into stocking our supermarket shelves, planned in meticulous detail right down to having computers calculate the most efficient speed at which trucks should travel on our roads.

Finally, prior to a brief look at the making of *Britain From Above*, *The future* gazes into the crystal ball of what Britain might be like in

LEFT: A British icon – JCB excavators in their distinctive yellow livery parked outside the factory in Warwickshire. Joseph Cyril Bamford founded the company that bears his initials in 1945 and it has since grown to become the world's third largest manufacturer of construction equipment, with factories in the UK, US, Brazil, Germany, India and China.
RIGHT: Teepees (aka tipis) and flags at Glastonbury 2008. Since the early years of the festival, the Tipi Field has been set aside for tipi-dwellers who travel to Glastonbury, which now boasts Europe's largest annual gathering of tipis. In recent years festival organiser Michael Eavis has arranged for more than a hundred tipis to be available for hire to non tipi-owners.

years to come. Architects' visualisations, computer-generated models and glimpses of the future in the recent past all provide clues as to how our cities, transport systems, countryside and farms might develop over the next fifty years.

Throughout this wide-ranging and varied portrait of Britain, one perspective ties everything together, shedding new light on the way we live, on the way we have shaped our landscape over thousands of years, and on the way the landscape and the climate have shaped us, the British people. That unifying perspective is the view of Britain from above.

Ian Harrison

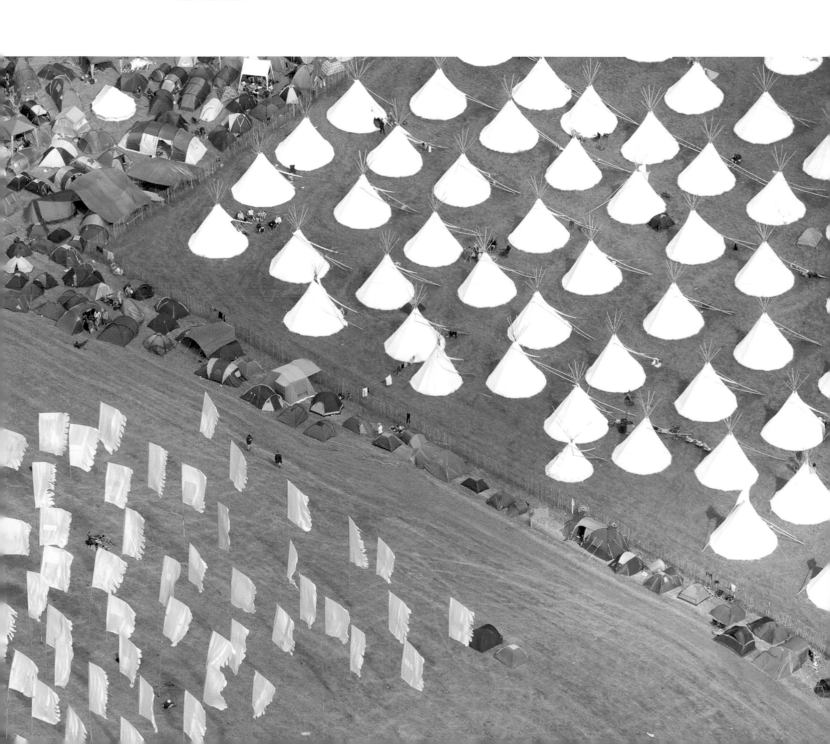

The rocks beneath
our feet

Britain's landscape is stunningly diverse, ranging from the crowded streets of its cities to the splendid isolation of its wildest places. Yet the thread linking all this diversity together is the rocks beneath our feet.

From above, satellite imagery reveals the amazing range of rock types that make up the UK – most spectacularly in Scotland's Great Glen, whose rocks once lay 30° south of the equator. Even more surprising, the rocks on one side of the Great Glen are 200 million years older than the rocks on the other. With mysteries like this hidden beneath its landscape, it is small wonder that the science of geology was pioneered in Scotland. It began with eighteenth-century geologists picking their way through the mountains on ponies and it continues today with their descendants poring over photographs taken from space.

The Great Glen – known in Scotland as *Gleann mor na-h Albyn*, or Glenmore Albyn – is part of a vast geological faultline running straight from Ireland to Shetland, and it contains one of Scotland's most famous landmarks, Loch Ness. Using enhanced satellite images of the rock types, geologists can now build a picture of how this part of Scotland came together some 4-500 million years ago. Rather than being a complete shell, the earth's crust is made up of huge rafts of rock known as tectonic plates, and the Caledonian mountains were formed when massive geological forces pushed two tectonic plates together. The plates that would become Europe and the Americas came together at a rate of a few centimetres a year, gradually closing the ocean that lay between them and eventually colliding along the line of the Great Glen. The force of this monumental collision was so great that it pushed billions of tons of rocks up into the air to form a mountain range as high as the Himalayas.

RIGHT: The conical peaks and U-shaped valley of Glen Coe are perfect examples of the effects of glaciation – the valley was gouged out of the rock by thousands of tons of ice and rock as the glacier inched its way towards lower ground. In the foreground is the summit of *Sgorr nam Fiannaidh* which faces the mass of *Aonoch Dubh* across the valley. The river Coe flows westward into Loch Achtriochtan between them. The area is protected by the National Trust for Scotland.

The reason Ben Nevis is no longer as high as Everest is simple – ice. The last Ice Age began some two million years ago, long after the European and American tectonic plates had moved apart again taking some of Scotland's rocks to Greenland and Canada. On five separate occasions glaciers made up of billions of tons of ice advanced across Britain, sometimes as far south as London. In Scotland this ice was up to a mile thick, and as it moved southwards it scoured the landscape, grinding down the mountains and gouging out features such as the glacial valleys that we see today. At the same time, as a result of so much water being frozen, sea levels fell by up to 100 metres. The North Sea was emptied, and when sea levels rose again water poured into many of the glaciated valleys to form the lochs of West Scotland. The fact that some of those lochs are 300 metres deep is an indication of the power of glacial erosion and how deeply it cut into the landscape.

From above, the Great Glen is like an open book telling the story of Scotland over hundreds of millions of years. But that book is not yet complete, because Scotland is still recovering from the effects of the Ice Age. Those billions of tons of ice pressing down on the landscape caused it to sink, and when the ice last retreated some 18,000 years ago the land began to rise again due to a process called glacial isostatic adjustment. That process is still going on today, and GPS (global positioning system) data shows that the land is rising at a rate of up to a centimetre per year. However, the most recent effect of the Ice Age has been social. In 1822 the Caledonian Canal was cut through the Great Glen, linking east and west Scotland to create new markets on both coasts.

The chalk uplands of the South Downs meet the Sussex coast in spectacular style at the Seven Sisters Country Park. In March 1999 Belle Tout lighthouse, in the foreground, was moved 17 metres back from the cliff edge to prevent it collapsing into the sea.

WHITE CLIFFS OF...

Just as the Caledonian mountains help define the character of Scotland, so the rolling hills of the southern chalk downlands have become the archetypal English landscape. England's topography changes dramatically along a diagonal line stretching from Exeter to Newcastle. The rocks to the north and west of this line are older and harder, creating a more rugged landscape than the rocks to the south and east which have eroded into gentler terrain characterised by long ridges, wide valleys and expansive plains. And in the south-east corner of England, formed by some of the youngest of all Britain's rocks, are the distinctive chalk downlands. It could be said that geology became part of the national psyche after Vera Lynn sang *The White Cliffs of Dover* (though they were hardly that white and the bluebird is non-native to the British Isles).

The chalk that makes up these rolling hills and sheer cliffs was formed by the shells and skeletons of countless sea creatures sinking to the beds of ancient oceans and being turned to stone by pressure. During the Cretaceous period (136-65 million years ago) chalk formed at a rate of one foot of chalk every 30,000 years, which means that it would have taken nearly 16 million years to form just the visible part of another of England's famous chalk landmarks, the 162-metre cliff of Beachy Head.

Chalk landscape is often referred to as downland or Downs, not because it is lower than the surrounding countryside but because the word is a corruption of a medieval word 'dun', meaning 'hill'. Downlands such as the Chilterns and the North and South Downs are formed when geological movement pushes the chalk up above the surrounding rocks, exposing it to the elements. Being a soft rock it erodes in smooth rolling hills rather than jagged formations, and because the chalk layer is usually tilted when it is raised up, the typical downland landscape forms in well-defined ridges with a steep slope on one side known as a scarp or escarpment, and a gentle slope on the other known as a dip. Chalk provides very fertile soil, so the hills are usually lush and green – until they meet the coast, where the sea undermines them to form sheer, strikingly white cliffs such as those at Flamborough, Seven Sisters and Beachy Head.

EXTRACTION ENGINES

The geological forces that formed Britain's varied landscape also produced immense riches in the rocks beneath our feet and off our shores. These treasures include the reserves of coal and iron ore that enabled Britain to become the first nation in the world to industrialise, as well as more recently discovered North Sea oil which has helped sustain the economy since the decline of heavy manufacturing. The UK's mineral resources even include gold, which was discovered during the 1980s in the 'Ulster Klondike'.

In 1983, whilst working in Northern Ireland for a mineral exploration company, Seamus Mullan and Garth Earls became the first men to discover bedrock gold in the UK for nearly two thousand years. Deposits known as alluvial gold have been found more recently in the sediment of streams and rivers, but this was the first time veins of gold-bearing rock had been discovered since the Romans found bedrock gold in Wales. Mullan and Earls discovered the gold in the traditional manner – by walking up a stream with gold pans and hammers – but they confirmed their find from the air. They noted that a stream running through the town of Gortin, County Tyrone, made several sudden changes of course, and by interpreting maps and aerial photographs of the stream they realised that the changes of course were caused by underground veins of quartz containing gold. The veins are known as the Curraghinalt resource, which has since been shown to contain an estimated 17 tons of gold. In January 2007 an open cast mine opened at Cavanacaw to begin mining the resource. It will remain the

BELOW: An open cast kaolin mine near St Austell, Cornwall. Until this resource was discovered in 1746 the only known deposits of high-grade kaolin were in China, hence the name china clay for kaolin and china for fine pottery and porcelain. Josiah Wedgwood was one of those who invested in Cornwall.
TOP RIGHT: One of the processes used for refining china clay is to allow impurities to settle out in large sedimentation tanks. Seen from above it is a colourful process in which the clay suspension changes hue as the different impurities settle.
BOTTOM RIGHT: The open cast gold mine at Cavanacaw, Northern Ireland, the UK's only gold mine. The gold mined here was formed when the European and American tectonic plates were still joined, which means that Ulster's gold is part of the same Canadian deposit that inspired the famous Klondike gold rush.

UK's only gold mine until an underground mine is opened at Gortin in the near future.

Britain is also rich in other resources whose value is less obvious but which have nonetheless proved important: vast seams of clay, which is used as a raw material for the billions of bricks that make up our homes; limestone, a raw material for the mortar that holds those bricks together; and even salt, which was vital for the survival of early humans, because for thousands of years it was mankind's only food preservative. Though no longer critical to the nation's survival, nearly two million tons of pure and rock salt is mined in Britain every year and used for cooking, chemical manufacturing and de-icing our roads in winter.

China clay was discovered in Cornwall in 1746 and gradually overtook tin and copper mining as the area's main industry. Some 120 million tons of china clay have been extracted, and there is still enough in the ground to last another hundred years.

CHINA CLAY

Open cast kaolin mining near St Austell, Cornwall. The mining process involves blasting the quarry face with high-pressure water cannon to form a slurry which runs down to the lowest part of the quarry, known as the sink. The slurry is then pumped back up to the 'sand classifiers' seen here, which remove the coarsest sand before the remaining clay suspension is piped to sedimentation tanks (see previous page) to be further refined. The coarse sand removed at the first stage is dumped in spoil heaps which are then grassed over (see page 24). The spoil heaps are extensive because mining produces far more spoil than kaolin – some nine tons of waste for every ton of china clay.

A NATION RISING AND FALLING

Mining the treasures beneath our feet has brought Britain untold wealth but there is a down side – subsidence. The hazards of exploiting our geology are well known to the 240,000 inhabitants of Stoke-on-Trent and to thousands of inhabitants of other former coal-mining towns and cities. Today, most of Britain's coal mines have been shut down and many of them have been grassed over or turned into housing estates. In many of these areas there is little visual evidence that mining was ever carried out there, but hundreds of years of tunnelling have left their legacy. Seventy square miles of coal seams were mined beneath Stoke-on-Trent, and since the mining stopped, the ground has begun to subside dramatically, creating cracks in the ground, making buildings unstable and causing church towers to lean like their Pisan cousin.

Recently scientists have found a method of measuring and mapping subsidence so that action can be taken to reduce the damage it causes – and this mapping is done from above. Permanent scatterer interferometry, or PSInSar™, is a satellite radar system that can measure with millimetre accuracy how much the ground is moving. The system uses radar to measure the precise distance between scattered fixed points, such as the corners of buildings. Data are collected at regular intervals as the satellite passes over the site again and again, and then compared in order to calculate the rate at which Britain's landscape and the ground under the nation's cities is shifting or sinking.

The surprising result of the North Staffordshire survey was not which parts of Stoke are subsiding but the fact that the ground over the northern part of the coalfield is rising rapidly, at up to 5 mm a year. Geologists think this is caused by water returning to the mineworks – water was pumped out when the mines were in use, causing shrinkage, but since the mining stopped, the rocks have become re-saturated, pushing up the ground above them. Physicist Sir Isaac Newton established that for every action there is an equal and opposite reaction, and it seems that his law applies even to mining: if we dig out the treasures from the rocks beneath our feet, the rocks will react, either by sinking or rising.

Westport Lake, the largest body of water in Stoke-on-Trent, is now part of a public park and local nature reserve supporting some 200 species of bird. Until the late nineteenth century this was Port Vale FC's practice ground. Then, in the 1890s, the pitch became waterlogged when the ground subsided due to deep undermining, forming the lake which is approximately 10 hectares in area but only one metre deep. The PSInSar™ image (left) shows that since mining stopped, the landscape around the lake has started rising – spots in green are stable, those in turquoise are rising at 0-2.5 mm per year, and those in blue at 2.5-5 mm per year.

Shaping the land

In its truly natural state, much of Britain was densely forested. When the glaciers receded at the end of the last Ice Age, trees rapidly set down roots and by 7,000 BC the whole of Britain was covered in a cloak of lime, oak and yew. This wildwood was so dense and complete it is said that an animal such as a squirrel could travel the length of Britain through the forest canopy without ever putting its feet on the ground. With such dense tree coverage there were few clear areas for farming, and mankind's first impact on the British landscape began when the first hunter-gatherers began clearing areas of forest to give themselves places to settle and to trap animals.

Deforestation accelerated rapidly with the advent of farming but forests have always remained a vital part of the British way of life. After the original wildwood was gone, large sections of the British landscape effectively became tree factories, planted to provide raw materials for the ships that discovered new continents and defended the nation's shores, and for the pit props vital to the mining that fuelled the industrial revolution.

But the problem with planting trees as a cash crop is that by the time the forest is ready to harvest, demand may have altered. Some of our oldest forests were planted in the early nineteenth century to provide timber for shipbuilding, and only remain today because they didn't mature until after wooden ships were superseded by iron and steel. During the First World War, so much timber was used for trench props and pit props that successive governments planted vast plantations of fast-growing pines which matured in time for a Second World War without trenches and a coal industry in permanent decline.

The same problem – trying to predict future need – still applies to current forestry policy. Now, pioneering aerial surveys are helping to shape the forests of the future, this time with climate change in mind. The total carbon content of the nation's trees is being measured from the air, so that in future, harvesting can be monitored and forests preserved or extended in order to maintain the nation's carbon balance.

PREVIOUS PAGE: The Iron Age hill fort of Old Sarum in Wiltshire has borne witness to more than two and a half millennia of landscape change since it was built around 500 BC. It was used by the Romans, the Saxons and then the Normans who built a cathedral, a palace and a castle within the earthworks. The settlement declined after the cathedral was replaced by one at New Sarum, now better known as Salisbury.

LEFT: The dense tree cover of the Forest of Dean gives some impression of what most of Britain looked like 9,000 years ago; but it is not all as ancient as it looks. The forest was designated a Royal Forest in the eleventh century but 500 years later Henry VIII had to order massive replanting because it had been over-exploited for ship-building timber, charcoal and the extraction of iron ore. The forest did not fully recover until the nineteenth century, when more replanting resulted in the modern forest of some 20 million trees – mainly oak, ash and silver birch.

RIGHT: The regimented lines of this commercially planted forest near Loch Duntelchaig in Scotland are a marked contrast with the more random nature of the Forest of Dean.

ABOVE AND RIGHT: Under the ancient strip farming system each family worked a narrow strip or strips of land in the fields near their village. In many places where the strips were separated by ditches or embankments, or where ploughing was done on a slope, ridges known as lynchets can still be seen today. The lynchets to the right are in the Northumberland National Park, south of the village of Ingram. In the mid-fourteenth century an increasing amount of land was used for pasture rather than cultivating crops, and small groups of strips were often enclosed by walls, as above at Chelmorton in Derbyshire, and passed into single ownership.

THE BIRTH OF FARMING

Every year, as the seasons change, traces of the ancient past appear in the light and shadows playing across our fields. They are only visible from above, in certain light conditions, but many of the ghostly shapes that emerge are the direct result of farming carried out by our ancestors. Soil drainage and root penetration are affected by the remains of ancient walls or foundations below ground, or ancient ditches filled with silt. When there are no crops or vegetation these otherwise invisible features may show up as light or dark patches where the soil drains more quickly or more slowly than the surrounding earth; in winter snow may melt slower or quicker; and crops will grow better in areas that retain moisture and worse in areas that drain too quickly or where root penetration is poor. Seen from the air when the sun is low, the difference between these more luxuriant or slightly stunted crops and the rest of the harvest reveals the shapes of ancient furrows, field enclosures and farm buildings of the past.

Since the first hunter-gatherers began clearing areas of forest to give themselves places to settle, farming and agriculture have shaped our landscape. Small-holdings were set aside for cultivating crops, and from about 800 AD until the fifteenth century an increasing amount of the British landscape was given over to strip farming. The land around towns and villages was divided into long strips, each about an acre in area, to create a truly communal farming system – each family was entitled to work a strip (or several separated strips) on which they could keep livestock and grow grain and vegetables.

During the Middle Ages our ancestors put more land under the plough than at any other time in Britain's history. Evidence of that phenomenally widespread farming can still be seen in the crumbling walls, dilapidated farmsteads and even abandoned villages that are scattered across what is now barren moorland as far afield as the moors of the West Country and the Highlands of Scotland. From the eighteenth century onwards farming became less extensive and more intensive. Instead of farming every inch of available land, the more fertile land was turned over to private landowners and 'enclosed' – fenced in behind

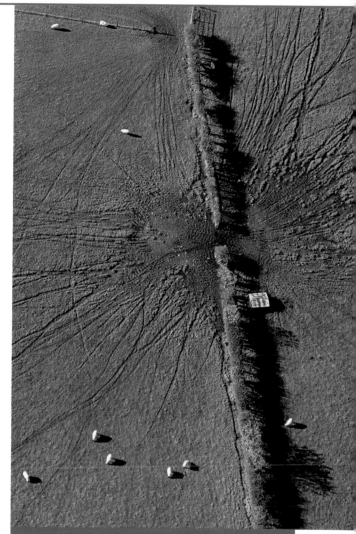

ABOVE: The Enclosure Movement of the eighteenth century introduced what many view as the distinctive element of the countryside in England and Wales – hedges. Private landowners enclosed open fields and common lands within hedges, walls and rows of trees. Many of the fields were enclosed using hawthorn or blackthorn. Hawthorn was the hedgerow of choice because it grew quickly and because it was particularly thorny and very effective at keeping in livestock. Ash, field maple, hazel and elm were also used because the stems could be partially cut and laid at an angle of 35 degrees and then woven between stakes driven into the ground.

hedges and walls, and divided into fields. This upheaval became known as the Enclosure Movement, and it angered Britain's peasants, who found that thick hedges of fast-growing hawthorn now cut them off from land they had once roamed at will.

A DWINDLING HEDGE FUND

Britain nearly starved during the Second World War. Farming methods had not advanced significantly since the nineteenth century and Britain produced barely 30 per cent of its own food, which meant that when supplies were cut off by the German U-boat blockade the nation struggled to feed itself. When the war ended the government embarked on a fabulously ambitious plan to revolutionise British agriculture and make the nation self-sufficient.

Farmers were given subsidies to mechanise and the government guaranteed fixed prices for certain crops. Tradition fell by the wayside – in place of labour-intensive mixed farming, farmers turned to fully mechanised farming of only the most profitable crops. Four combine harvesters could do the work of eighty horses, and manpower was reduced by more than a

RIGHT AND BELOW: At first glance the modern colour picture of the Huntingdon countryside appears to be a close-up version of the 1940s black and white one. But comparing the size of the village to the bottom left of both pictures, or the square patch of woodland at the centre of both, reveals that they both show the same location at the same scale – the difference is that thousands of metres of hedgerow have been removed in the intervening years, making the fields in the modern picture some five to ten times bigger than those of the 1940s.

factor of ten. It was a drastic policy, but it worked – food production rose by 50 per cent in the 1940s alone, and by the 1990s there was 300 per cent more food being produced per acre than in the 1930s. And as farming methods changed, so did Britain's rural landscape.

Between 1940 and 2000 the number of farms halved, as small farms were taken over by larger ones. Farmhouses and farm buildings disappeared as there were fewer farms and fewer people working them; and the number and width of roads increased to accommodate the new machinery. Most significantly, field sizes increased between five- and ten-fold, and changed shape from roughly oblong to strictly rectilinear to make them easier for tractors to plough. Subsidised by the Government, farmers drained their ponds and marshes, swept away woodland and hedges, and created an open landscape on which tractors and combine harvesters could work almost from horizon to horizon.

But what began as a purely agricultural process became a matter of national concern when the devastating effect on Britain's trees and hedges was made public. It is now estimated that between 1930 and 2000 no less than half of Britain's ancient woodland and eighteenth-century hedgerow was eradicated, and removing the hedgerows has now proved as controversial as planting them in the first place.

FARMING FROM ABOVE

In the twenty-first century, mechanised farming doesn't just mean tractors and combine harvesters – it includes cutting-edge military technology such as remote-controlled UAVs (unmanned aerial vehicles), satellite imagery, GPS (global positioning system) and computerised self-steering farm vehicles. For thousands of years farmers have only been able to get a very limited perspective on their land. Unless there was a convenient hill or tall building overlooking their fields the only way they could check their crops was to walk among them – until now. CropCam is a lightweight UAV which is essentially a spy plane specially modified for precision agriculture, and it allows farmers to survey their crops from above. It follows a pre-programmed flightplan fed into it from a laptop, and can cover 160 acres in twenty minutes, taking high resolution digital images of the fields below which tell the farmer exactly which areas need reseeding or additional fertiliser.

Elsewhere in the UK, farmers are taking the new agricultural revolution beyond the skies into space. Some of Britain's largest farms are in Suffolk, where millions of tons of grain are produced in fields the size of a small town. Computer analysis of satellite images can create a detailed map pinpointing differences in soil fertility down to a few centimetres. Before the advent of this technology, farmers would apply the same amount of fertiliser over an entire field but now they know where it is needed most – except that on the ground it is almost impossible for tractor drivers to locate the less fertile areas accurately by eye, so the operation is handled automatically by driverless tractors. Data from the satellite imagery are converted into GPS coordinates and fed into computers on board the tractors, and the computers then take over the entire operation – steering the tractors across the fields and spreading fertiliser in the exact amounts and locations required. Tending the land, one of our nation's oldest skills, has been handed over to robots.

THE MAN-MADE NORFOLK BROADS

For thousands of years, agriculture and industry have shaped Britain's landscape. Often these changes have established themselves so firmly in the collective consciousness that they seem perfectly natural. Britain's pattern of hedgerows – artificially and controversially introduced for eighteenth-century agricultural improvement – are now so firmly entrenched in the national psyche that it proved just as controversial when they were removed for twentieth-century agricultural purposes.

An even more surprising example is the Norfolk Broads, which for hundreds of years were regarded as natural features of the landscape. It was not until the 1960s that archaeologists proved them to be an artificial feature – the result of flooding on early peat excavations.

The Romans first exploited the rich peat beds of the area for fuel, and in the Middle Ages the local monasteries excavated peat in the same area, making vast profits by selling it as fuel to the inhabitants of Norwich and Great Yarmouth. But unfortunately for the monasteries the peat bonanza, like all good things, came to an end. Sea levels rose and the peat beds began to flood. Despite the construction of windmills and dykes the flooding continued, resulting in the Broads landscape, with its reed beds and grazing marshes, that is so familiar today. For the next few centuries the Broads acted as a trade route for shipping goods around East Anglia, but with the coming of the railways commerce and trade dried up. Tourism took over and the area became one of Britain's favourite destinations for day-trippers and families seeking a boating holiday.

In the 1980s and 1990s ecological catastrophe hit the Broads – the water became murky and the flora and fauna of the Broads began to die. The problem was largely due to phosphates from industrial farming leaching into the water. Since then, the Broads Authority has used groundbreaking techniques to remove the phosphates and turn the Broads into an example of successful eco-management, with dozens of species of birds and animals returning to the area. Norfolk has always had to maintain a balance between agriculture, tourism and nature. Ironically, while the Broads Authority has re-established the balance, it may soon be upset again by nature – despite extensive marine defences the whole area could disappear under the sea within decades.

STRANGLED BY THE CITY

The vast industrial landscape that stretches across the north of England from Liverpool on the west coast to Hull on the east, is home to a higher concentration of people than almost any other region in Europe. At its heart are the industrial cities of Manchester, Leeds and Sheffield, all crowding in on an oasis of undeveloped land – the Peak District National Park. The Park is being slowly asphyxiated by the pollution these cities have churned out since the Industrial Revolution, but recently conservationists have found a way of reversing the damage – from the air.

The Peak District comprises 555 square miles of beautiful and often wild countryside. It is one of the world's most visited National Parks, but the heather moorlands that are the defining feature of this part of northern England are being systematically poisoned. They are patchy, unhealthy and in need of repair after more than 200 years of pollution has destroyed the mosses which form peat, making it difficult for other vegetation to grow. This in turn makes the landscape more vulnerable to the elements – where the peat is laid bare the frost lifts the top layer, loosening it and speeding up erosion by the wind and rain, which creates deep gulleys down which yet more peat is washed away in a vicious circle that weakens the remaining vegetation.

To prevent further soil erosion and to enable plant species to recover, the peat needs to be stabilised. This is being done by 'reseeding' the moorland with heather and various carefully selected grasses, and it is such a massive project that the only way to do it is from above, by helicopter. First granulated lime is spread over the moorland to reduce the acidity of the soil. Then grass seed, heather seed and fertiliser are scattered over the damaged landscape, using GPS to plot the optimum track for the helicopter in order to maximise the seed coverage. The plan is that the grass (which likes a less acidic soil and which establishes quicker than heather) will put roots down in the peat and knit everything together, reducing further erosion. This will create a more stable environment in which the heather will be able to re-establish itself; at this point liming will stop and the soil will begin to acidify again. The reseeding project may take several years but the plan is that this mechanical intervention will return the landscape to a more natural state which will be capable of sustaining itself.

RIGHT: The semi-wild landscape of the Peak District National Park is hemmed in by one of the most densely populated industrial regions in Europe. Pollution is gradually killing off the vegetation, evidence of which lies in the bare patches of earth visible in the foreground.
LEFT: An ambitious project is under way to repair the pollution damage by reseeding the moorland in order to halt the vicious circle of diminishing vegetation and soil erosion, each exacerbating the other. This is such a massive task in such a vulnerable habitat, that it can only be undertaken by helicopter.

SHAPING THE LAND FOR LEISURE

The Peak District National Park was founded in 1951 as Britain's first National Park. It was the result of far-sighted legislation to protect massive areas of the British countryside from development and from unsightly agricultural or industrial exploitation. When the National Parks and Access to the Countryside Act was passed in 1949 Lewis Silkin, Minister for Town and Country Planning, called it 'the most exciting Act of the post-war Parliament.' This momentous Act paved the way for the creation of fourteen National Parks which now cover 8,862 square miles of Britain, with a fifteenth under consideration – the 1,020 square miles of the South Downs which, if designated a National Park, will bring the total to nearly 10,000 square miles. In England and Scotland, National Parks comprise 7 per cent and 7.3 per cent of the land area respectively, while the three National Parks in Wales make up a massive 20 per cent of the Welsh land area.

RIGHT: Opening in 1980, Alton Towers has become Britain's largest amusement park and one of the nation's most popular tourist destinations, attracting almost two and a half million visitors a year.

BELOW: Although the National Parks exist to preserve a seemingly wild, natural landscape, it is not always as natural as it seems. Even these protected areas have been shaped by man, from the very obvious car parks, visitor centres and footpaths that serve modern visitors to subtler or more ancient interventions such as Neolithic forest clearance, the action of livestock grazing on the hillsides, and the building of dry stone walls. The Peak District, pictured here, contains 8,756 kilometres of dry stone walls. It was the appearance of dry stone walls in the Lake District that led the poet William Wordsworth to pre-empt the idea of National Parks by suggesting that government should preserve 'a sort of national property' for everyone to enjoy.

Each Park Authority is responsible for conserving and enhancing the natural beauty, wildlife and cultural heritage of its designated area, but appreciating the British countryside is not just about conserving the semi-wild landscape of the National Parks and other protected areas such as sites of outstanding natural beauty, special areas of conservation, and sites of special scientific interest. Much of our rural and coastal landscape has been

LEFT: In many parts of Britain where holidaymakers flock to the coast, vast areas of land are given over to camp sites, caravan parks and serried ranks of holiday chalets like this holiday village near Woolacombe in Devon.

BELOW: In 1987 CenterParcs changed the British holiday market and the British landscape with the first of its forest-based holiday villages, which opened at Sherwood Forest in Nottinghamshire. CenterParcs now runs four villages in British forests, each of about 400 acres, including this one which opened in 1997 in Whinfell Forest in the Lake District. Hidden among the trees are 773 lodges and seventy-nine apartments capable of accommodating up to 4,668 guests. The park also has a watersports lake and restaurants, shops, bars and sports facilities in the glass-covered 'Village Centre'.

specifically and extensively shaped for leisure activities, including the massive acreage set aside for golf courses, race courses, motor racing circuits, marinas, caravan and camp sites, holiday camps, CenterParcs holiday villages, leisure parks and theme parks.

The vast amount of money spent on protecting the semi-wild areas and shaping other areas for leisure is money well spent, because tourism is one of the UK's biggest industries. The British countryside and coastline are such a draw for tourists, day-trippers and holidaymakers that tourism provides more than two million jobs and boosts the UK economy by some £85 billion a year – 80 per cent from domestic tourism and the rest from more than 32 million overseas visitors, most of whom visit from the USA, France and Germany.

A SYMBOLIC LANDSCAPE

Stonehenge is one of Britain's true mysteries – this majestic triple stone circle is world famous, yet no one knows who built it, nor when, why or how. For many years archaeologists thought it was built c2100 BC but recent evidence suggests that the monument we see today was built in three phases c3100 BC, c2100 BC and c1550 BC. How an ancient people could have transported scores of 40-ton bluestone blocks to Wiltshire from the Preseli mountains in Wales remains a mystery, as does the purpose of this great monument. Theories include ritual sacrifice, royal burial, sun worship, an astronomical clock, or the site of a symbolic marriage between the sun god and the Earth Mother – evidence for the last theory is that the sun rising over the Heel Stone is said to cast a phallic shadow into the inner sanctum.

DECORATING THE LANDSCAPE

The Uffington White Horse is not flat, but a 3D model made up of chalk blocks embedded a metre deep in the Wiltshire hillside. When archaeologists dug down and tested part of the horse's mouth they dated this amazing piece of art to between 1400 and 600 BC, making it about 3,000 years old. It can only be seen in its entirety from above, so whoever created it would never have been able to judge its proportions by eye. Much younger but equally imposing is Antony Gormley's Angel of the North, which stands 20 metres tall overlooking the road and rail routes into Tyneside. The Angel comprises 200 tons of steel and 600 tons of concrete foundations with a wingspan of 54 metres – almost as wide as that of a Jumbo jet.

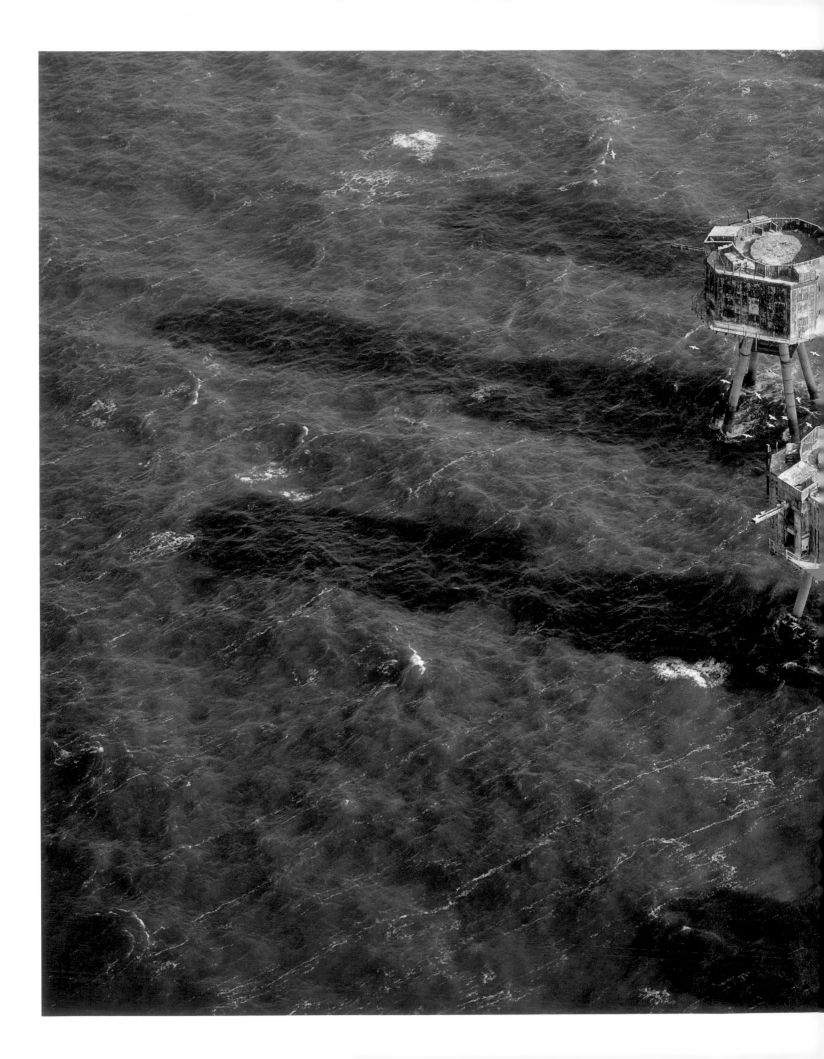

Hidden Britain

ABOVE: Munitions bunkers at DM Kineton, Warwickshire, which is one of several Defence Munitions sites in the UK. This is just a small part of the 2,500-acre site at Kineton, which includes 200 buildings, 21 miles of railway track for moving the munitions, and a 22-mile perimeter fence. Kineton's military connections were established long before modern munitions – the site also includes historic graves from the first major battle of the English Civil War, which took place in 1642 at nearby Edgehill.

RIGHT: Maunsell Army Forts. During the Second World War engineer Guy Maunsell designed two types of prefabricated fort which were towed out to sea on floating pontoons and then sunk so they came to rest on sandbanks with the superstructure above sea level. Three 'army forts' were deployed as anti-aircraft emplacements in the Mersey and three in the Thames estuary, one of which – 'Red Sands' – is seen here. Each fort comprised seven platforms: a control centre and accommodation tower surrounded by five gun towers, with a searchlight tower set slightly further apart, all linked by walkways which have since been removed.

Until recently, surprisingly large amounts of the British countryside were officially hidden from the public, but many of these secret areas are now being revealed – from above.

Britain's second largest landowner, after the Forestry Commission, is the Ministry of Defence which owns some 4,000 sites covering 600,000 acres of the British landscape. These sites include undeveloped woods, plains, lakes and moorland, as well as some 45,000 buildings ranging from barracks, bunkers, munitions dumps and fake villages to naval bases, aircraft hangars, radar stations and historic buildings. As recently as the last decade a large number of MoD sites were simply missing from Ordnance Survey maps, but the government has changed its policy on 'sensitive sites' because their whereabouts have been revealed by publicly available satellite imagery, Soviet Cold War maps and other sources.

Post Office worker Alan Turnbull has made an alternative career out of locating semi-secret MoD sites by investigating mapping anomalies and by correlating internet satellite images against Ordnance Survey maps, then posting his findings on his popular website, www.secret-bases.co.uk. He searches satellite images and aerial photographs for features that are unmistakable from above but which don't appear on the maps, then investigates what's there and why it's been left off the map. For instance, when he noticed what appeared to be a new housing estate in the middle of the Warwickshire countryside he looked more closely and discovered that it was actually a fake street built at the Defence Munitions Headquarters, DM Kineton, as a training facility for bomb disposal.

Turnbull has also become an expert at reading the empty spaces on Ordnance Survey maps. As recently as 2005 his suspicions were raised by a map showing a road which came to a dead end at the edge of what appeared to be an unusually large field. Satellite imagery revealed a large installation which proved to be the Atomic Weapons Establishment base at Burghfield in Berkshire, which has since appeared on the latest maps.

ABOVE AND RIGHT: Lydd Range (above) and Hythe Range (right) are fake villages built on the beaches of the Kent coast as part of the MoD's Cinque Ports Training Area. They are live firing ranges for training army, navy and air force personnel in urban warfare. Judging by the posters of Saddam Hussein and the sign advertising Abdul's Cafe in the smaller picture, Hythe has been used for training troops destined for Iran and Afghanistan. The ranges are used on some 300 days a year and timetables are sent to local harbour masters, sailing clubs and coastguard stations so that seafarers can avoid the danger areas.

ABOVE: Mock-up of detached houses and terraced streets at the Defence Munitions Headquarters in Warwickshire. This life-size street frontage, complete with parked cars, was built in 2006 as an 'improvised explosive device disposal training centre' – or, in English, a school for defusing car bombs and booby traps. The centre is used to train NATO forces and Explosive Ordnance Disposal technicians (formerly known as bomb disposal experts) from the nearby Army School of Ammunition. It is known as the Felix Centre because, like cats, EOD technicians are said to need nine lives.

MENWITH HILL

Five of the twenty-plus radomes at 'RAF' Menwith Hill in North Yorkshire. Despite its official name, the controversial base at Menwith Hill is not run by the RAF but by the US National Security Agency, to whom it is known as Field Station F83. During the Cold War Menwith Hill and RAF Fylingdales were used as early warning stations to track Soviet nuclear missiles, but whereas the radomes at Fylingdales have since been dismantled, the 'golf balls' at Menwith Hill have multiplied more than six-fold. BBC News has described the installation as the largest electronic monitoring station in the world. The base appears on the latest Ordnance Survey maps but for many years OS maps showed only empty fields.

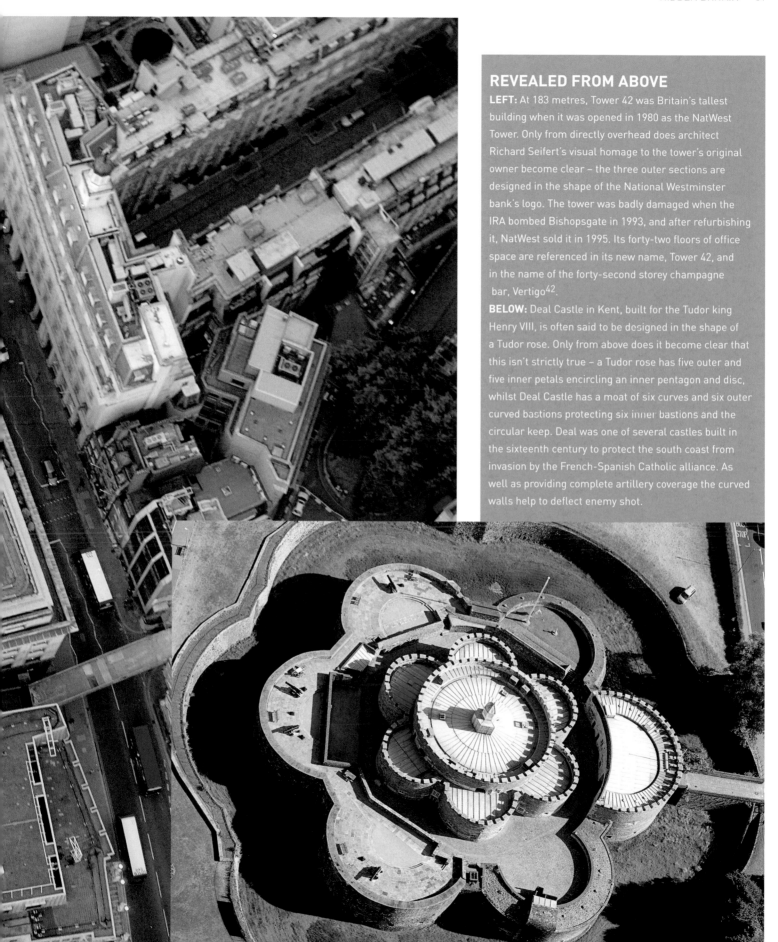

REVEALED FROM ABOVE

LEFT: At 183 metres, Tower 42 was Britain's tallest building when it was opened in 1980 as the NatWest Tower. Only from directly overhead does architect Richard Seifert's visual homage to the tower's original owner become clear – the three outer sections are designed in the shape of the National Westminster bank's logo. The tower was badly damaged when the IRA bombed Bishopsgate in 1993, and after refurbishing it, NatWest sold it in 1995. Its forty-two floors of office space are referenced in its new name, Tower 42, and in the name of the forty-second storey champagne bar, Vertigo[42].

BELOW: Deal Castle in Kent, built for the Tudor king Henry VIII, is often said to be designed in the shape of a Tudor rose. Only from above does it become clear that this isn't strictly true – a Tudor rose has five outer and five inner petals encircling an inner pentagon and disc, whilst Deal Castle has a moat of six curves and six outer curved bastions protecting six inner bastions and the circular keep. Deal was one of several castles built in the sixteenth century to protect the south coast from invasion by the French-Spanish Catholic alliance. As well as providing complete artillery coverage the curved walls help to deflect enemy shot.

RIGHT: A crop circle at Furze Knoll, Hampshire, reported in June 2008. Crop circles became a fashionable phenomenon in the 1980s but scientists had been recording them for at least a century before that. In 1880 the journal *Nature* published a report describing the after-effects of a storm in Surrey: 'we found a field of standing wheat considerably knocked about, not as an entirety, but in patches forming, as viewed from a distance, circular spots... They were to me suggestive of some cyclonic wind action...' More than 10,000 crop circles have been recorded around the world, a high percentage of which have been revealed as hoaxes or works of art. But, like UFOs, they have not all been satisfactorily explained and some people believe they are supernatural in origin.

BELOW: A crop maze in Kent. Humans have been devising mazes and labyrinths since ancient times. The earliest mazes were built as symbolic traps for malevolent spirits, while medieval ones often represented symbolic pilgrimages, with the various paths symbolising the moral choices to be made on the journey towards God. Later, the religious significance faded and mazes were built purely for entertainment.

SAVERNAKE FOREST

Savernake Forest near Marlborough contains some of the oldest trees in Britain, but although it may look like the last remnant of the dense wildwoods that covered the country 9,000 years ago it is nowhere near that old – most of these trees were planted in the nineteenth century. However, the forest does contain some traces of the ancient past; clues which are hidden beneath the trees and, surprisingly, can only be seen from above. It is difficult for archaeologists to research the history of wooded landscapes using traditional methods because the trees and undergrowth prevent any detailed surveying. Now, however, using state-of-the-art military technology known as LiDAR (Light Detection and Ranging), it has become possible to survey forested areas from the air. Airborne LiDAR, which works on a similar principle to radar, was originally invented in the 1960s for submarine detection but only in the twenty-first century did it become sufficiently well developed to allow archaeologists to start mapping land covered by forests. LiDAR fires rapid laser pulses at the ground from about 3,000 feet and measures the time it takes for the reflected light to return to the onboard computer. The time delay of each pulse is used to calculate distance and create a digital surface model of the land – and what makes LiDAR so special is that it can distinguish between the laser light reflecting off leaves and the light reflecting from the ground, providing aerial archaeologists with images that strip away the tree cover and reveal the landscape below.

LiDAR images of Savernake Forest reveal that although this extraordinary woodland is prized for its wild and natural state, it is actually the cover for a number of man-made creations including a Second World War munitions dump, a series of medieval tracks, a Roman road, Roman pottery kilns and, oldest of all, an Iron Age temple (visible as a square enclosure in the centre of the right-hand image) – evidence that there was a settlement here as long ago as 700 BC.

London skyline

Like nearly all of Britain's cities London wasn't planned – it grew organically. City Design professor Bill Hillier explains that although we think of our cities as manmade and artificial they expand with a life of their own. Roads ribbon out from the centre, smaller roads spider out from the main roads, the smaller roads connect with each other and so the city keeps on expanding, through evolution and adaptation rather than through planning. 'If I were creating a new city,' says Hillier, 'I wouldn't design one. I'd grow one.'

And so it was with London. The nation's capital started as a Roman settlement at the lowest fordable point on the Thames and has been growing haphazardly ever since. From above it becomes clear just how much the capital's distant past has affected its development right up to the present – for instance, the Guildhall is built on the site of a Roman amphitheatre and the modern street alignments still echo the curvature of that ancient building, while the 'accidental geometry' of the weblike maze of lanes and alleyways at the heart of the City of London has changed little since the Middle Ages.

As the capital grew it expanded in linear fashion, east and west along the Thames, hence the terms West End and East End. Then, with the growth of the suburbs made possible by the arrival of the railways, it expanded more conventionally – outwards from the centre. Architectural historian Paul Finch describes this as a biological process: 'London's fingers move out into the countryside. It doesn't move out block by block, and the consequence is that if you look at London from above, it has a series of almost fractal edges to it. It's not a disc, it's not a square, it's not an oblong – it's an organic, almost fish-like thing which extends its tentacles whenever it needs to. That's its true tradition.'

It is ironic that although London grew organically, many of its features are now protected by stringent planning regulations that control and protect the heritage of its skyline – most famously, St Paul's Cathedral is protected from being obscured by high buildings, not just for viewers in the immediate vicinity but along eight major viewing corridors from vantage points as far afield as Richmond and Kenwood. City planners assert that while the City of London may have evolved organically for some 2,000 years, in future it will evolve through planning – and for them, planning is as much about conservation as development. Developers often exert pressure to remove the ancient twists and turns of the City's lanes and streets to make space for more office blocks but, says

one planner: 'The City's planning polices are very strong in retaining the best of the past because they are important to our future. If the City's past were to be obliterated and rebuilt by developers it would just be like Canary Wharf.'

Planners strive to retain the best of the past but sometimes greater forces come into play. The chance of planning London afresh – doing away with the past and beginning again on a grand scale – has arisen twice in the capital's history, both after substantial disasters. The first was the Great Fire of 1666, when Sir Christopher Wren proposed ambitious plans for remodelling the entire City of London based on rational grids of lanes lying between long, straight, wide boulevards radiating out from circular piazzas. But in the end people rebuilt their property on the old medieval plan, and the only part of Wren's vision which came to fruition was St Paul's Cathedral, which gives a magnificent glimpse of what might have been. The second opportunity came after the devastation wrought by the Luftwaffe during the Blitz.

BELOW LEFT AND RIGHT: St Paul's Cathedral in 1948 (right) and in the 1950s. Seen from above, the extent of the Second World War devastation that surrounds St Paul's reveals just how miraculous it was that the cathedral wasn't destroyed. This was thanks in large measure to the St Paul's Watch, a group of 300 volunteers who included the poet John Betjeman and members of the Royal Institute of British Architects. Forty members of the Watch guarded St Paul's on each night of the Blitz ready to extinguish any incendiary devices that landed on or near the cathedral. Two bombs did penetrate St Paul's, damaging the crypt and destroying the Victorian high altar, and on 29 December an incendiary broke through the dome but was successfully extinguished by the Watch.

BELOW: Luftwaffe bombers follow the course of the Thames to unload their bombs over central London. The planes are over Plumstead Marshes, which is at the top of the picture, and Dagenham, with the Ford Motor Works visible in the extreme bottom left.

On the afternoon of 7 September 1940 three hundred Axis bombers attacked London. That night 180 more bombed the capital, and for seventy-six consecutive nights – apart from 2 November when bad weather grounded the Luftwaffe – an average of 200 bombers mercilessly pounded the capital. By 14 November, when the Germans temporarily moved the focus of the Blitz to Birmingham, Bristol, Coventry, Liverpool, Plymouth and Southampton, the Luftwaffe had dropped more than 13,000 tons of high explosives and nearly one million incendiaries on London, destroying docks, railway stations, power stations, gas works and residential areas.

The worst was over, but during the next six months – in addition to extending its attacks to Belfast, Clydeside, Humberside, Merseyside and Tyneside – the Luftwaffe dropped a further 7,000 tons of high explosives and thousands more incendiaries on the capital, culminating in a devastating attack on 10 May 1941 that left fires raging from Romford to Hammersmith. The Blitz on London killed 20,000 people, destroyed or damaged more than half the capital's housing stock, left 1.5 million people homeless, and devastated 225 acres of the ancient City of London – about one third of its entire area. And through it all St Paul's Cathedral, which had risen out of the ashes of the Great Fire, became a beacon of hope for the entire nation, miraculously surviving the Blitz despite the almost complete devastation that surrounded it.

THE ABERCROMBIE PLAN

As early as 1943, with the Second World War still raging, architect and town planner Sir Patrick Abercrombie, and colleague J.H. Forshaw, published their grand vision for the post-war rebuilding of London. But the 'Abercrombie Plan' was far more than just a scheme for replacing what had been destroyed – it was an attempt to regenerate people's spirits and to redefine how they could and should live in the city, even how the city itself should function. Abercrombie spelt out his bold vision in Churchillian style by announcing: 'We have an urgent duty to give the people of London new homes but, more than that, new hope for the future in a new city.'

Unlike modern London planners, who talk of retaining the past because it is important to the future, Abercrombie talked about banishing the past and embracing the future in its place; about building an entirely new metropolis laid out on more rational, egalitarian lines, with open roads and public spaces in place of the medieval pattern of old. Above all, it would be a clean, modern design: 'We will do away with

the old and bring in the new. And we must be brave because there will always be those who are afraid of change. But the changes we envisage will liberate the people of London...'

However, it is not clear that Abercrombie's plan would have liberated people. He proposed re-ordering London into zones in the name of efficiency: zones for living, for working, for retail, for commerce and for industry. At the heart of his plan was an admirable desire to give people space and freedom – for every thousand inhabitants, there was to be at least four acres of open green space; roughly twice as much as exists today. But in order to liberate these green spaces, vast tracts of property would have to be compulsorily purchased and the people themselves would have to be 'decentralised' (compulsorily moved out of the central zones) or housed in new tower blocks, stacked in rows across the city.

The Abercrombie Plan was not restricted to housing and green spaces – he also had bold plans for a road network that would transform London from an aging warren of old, grey

LEFT AND ABOVE: The Royal Festival Hall (RFH) in the 1950s and in 2008. The RFH is the only extant glimpse of what Abercrombie's London might have looked like. It is the only building to have survived from the South Bank Festival which was held here in 1951 as part of the nationwide Festival of Britain. Other features of the festival included the Dome of Discovery, which stood on the circle at the top of the archive photograph, and the Skylon Tower which stood in front of the Dome close to where the London Eye is now. The brick tower in the archive image is a nineteenth-century shot tower, which was used for making ammunition by dropping molten lead from the top so that it solidified as it fell.

THE SOUTH BANK

streets into a fast-moving paradise for cars.
Abercrombie assumed that the working classes
would live in the new high-rise estates in the
inner city while the middle classes would
commute in from satellite towns and the
suburbs. And in order for the middle classes
to do that he planned a vast network of wide
roads cutting right through the city – or over
it, or under it, caring little for what would
have to be swept out of the way in the process.
Plans included a fly-over across the Strand,
a motorway through Hoxton and Islington
along the north side of the Regent's Canal,
and tunnels beneath Bloomsbury and St
James's Park – all in an age when barely
10 per cent of Londoners owned a car and
petrol was still rationed.

Such was the hope for the future, it was
assumed that with enough political will
Abercrombie's dream could be realised.
However, it was not to be. Just as St Paul's
Cathedral provides a glimpse of what Sir
Christopher Wren's London might have looked
like, the Royal Festival Hall is the only major
example of what Abercrombie's London might
have looked like. His housing plans were barely
realised, and Burgess Park in Southwark is one
of the few remnants of his plans to double the
amount of green space. With the exception of
the M11 the nearest we have come to his grand
plan for the roads is the completion of the north
and south circular routes and the building of
the arterial routes that sweep towards London
before grinding to a near halt as they reach the
edges of the metropolis.

LEFT AND BELOW: Abercrombie's vision for the South
Bank of the Thames viewed from near the Savoy Hotel
(below) and the area in 2008. Abercrombie's design
proposes a new bridge at Temple, which was never
built, and a new road bridge where Hungerford Bridge
currently carries the railway into Charing Cross Station.
He also proposed a riverside walk from County Hall to
London Bridge which has become partial reality – there
is now pedestrian access along this stretch of riverside,
passing new buildings including the London Eye, Royal
Festival Hall, Hayward Gallery, Royal National Theatre,
Tate Modern and Shakespeare's Globe, as well as
Borough Market and numerous cafés and restaurants.

Abercrombie predicted that 'there will always
be those who fear change'. But in the end it
wasn't fear that scuppered his plans, it was
lack of funds. Architectural historian Paul Finch
believes that London as a city will always resist
grand plans, but he approves of Abercrombie's
intentions: 'I liked the modernist version
of London as an idea. Opening up the city,
giving people more room, cleaner, greener
neighbourhoods was a very noble aim. But to
do that, and to get all those great highways
ploughed through the city, would have meant
compulsorily buying out all the owners. Just as
Wren discovered 300 years earlier, there were
just too many of them to afford it, never mind
the cost of actual construction. Looking back
it was totally unrealistic. After the war Britain
was bankrupt and in debt to the US. There
was basically no public money for such grand
public schemes.'

RISING SKYLINE

After the Second World War Abercrombie was not the only person with plans for redeveloping London. The London County Council had plans, and so did the local authorities, but in the end all these plans suffered the same fate – individual landowners and developers refused to be dictated to and set about redeveloping their own patch in their own way. Or, as architectural historian Paul Finch puts it: 'The reason that a grand plan couldn't be imposed on London was because London is resistant to grand plans. What London responds to is trade, commerce, money, markets, prosperity. The biggest planning ideas in London have been underground – Bazalgette's sewerage system and the London underground system. Above ground it's cash that counts.'

The biggest change in the London skyline since the war is the height of the buildings. It is an obvious fact but the reason behind it is less obvious – London is built on clay, and until the 1960s the technology to build tall buildings in clay did not exist. When the Post Office Tower (now BT Tower) was opened in 1966 it was Britain's tallest building, and a unique addition to London's low-rise skyline. By the time the NatWest Tower (now Tower 42) took over as Britain's tallest building in 1980, London was growing into a mid-rise city. And by 1991, when One Canada Square (better known as the Canary Wharf Tower) took over as Britain's tallest building, London had some 300 buildings of more than twelve storeys. High-rise towers were becoming a characteristic of the London skyline

rather than an exception to it, giving London a new grandeur and scale. 'The result,' says Paul Finch, 'is that London is gradually, metre by metre, establishing itself as the world financial centre. I think twenty-five years ago there was a danger that it would become a bit of a museum piece.'

The City's capacity for physical growth has been limited by its historic shape, which means that for post-war architects the only way is up – a constraint which has resulted in some of the most striking designs in British architecture.

Among those designs are no fewer than seven new skyscrapers which are set to make a dramatic change to the London skyline in the next few years. These include the forty-eight-storey Leadenhall Building, designed by Richard Rogers, which will become the City's

tallest building when it opens in 2011. Because of its striking wedge-shaped profile, it has already been nicknamed 'The Cheese Grater', but the reason behind the design has more to do with respecting the history of the City skyline.

Rogers, who also designed the Millennium Dome and the world-famous Lloyd's Building, points out: 'Tall buildings – if sensitively inserted and designed – can function well, especially office buildings built as part of a cluster where the space between towers can be as important as the building itself, the cluster enriching the city and the skyline. One needs only to look at the skylines of Chicago and San Gimignano to be convinced. The winding medieval streets, defining irregular plot sizes, can lead to more dramatic building forms than the grid plan – for example, Washington.

ABOVE AND RIGHT: The Shard London Bridge. Designed by the Italian architect Renzo Piano, the Shard is set to become Britain's tallest building at 310 metres, and briefly the tallest in the European Union if it is completed before the 318-metre Tour Generali in Paris; both are scheduled for completion in 2011. The Shard will include a public viewing gallery near the top, which is expected to attract some two million visitors per year.

Another constraint is the conservation of view corridors to historic buildings. The Leadenhall Building – developed by British Land and designed by Rogers Stirk Harbour & Partners – responds to the view of St Paul's by sloping back to get out of the view.'

Thanks to designs like this the London skyline is now one of the most vibrant in the world. Architects and historians agree that this is because the skyline is not a grand design imposed on the capital by government-appointed visionaries like Abercrombie, but the result of market forces. To give the last word to Paul Finch: 'London has always been a city of markets. The fruit and vegetable and fish markets have moved further out to make way for the growing financial and insurance markets but the money is always there. The markets change but there are still markets. The day that the City of London isn't a market it won't be the City of London.'

LEFT AND ABOVE: Architects' visualisation of the 225 metre Leadenhall Tower, better known as the Cheese Grater (left), and (above) a photorealistic computer-generated image of how the Cheese Grater will look in situ as part of the London skyline. Unusually, the existing 1960s tower at Leadenhall Street is being demolished from the bottom up to make way for the Cheese Grater – its fifteen floors hang from a beam supported by a central concrete core, and the weight must be removed from the beam before the core can be demolished conventionally, from the top down.

CHANGING RIVERSCAPE

London's exact origins are unclear, but what is certain is that since people first settled on the banks of this part of the Thames more than 2,000 years ago, the river has been the city's lifeblood. It has helped London grow and thrive, providing water for drinking and washing, fish for food, power for mills, a highway for transporting people and goods, and most importantly a tidal port for international trade and commerce.

London has always been a port, and by 1700 the city's docks were handling 80 per cent of the country's imports and 69 per cent of its exports. By the 1920s the Royal Docks were the largest enclosed dock system in the world, covering 245 acres and served by nearly nine miles of quayside. Together with the other docks downstream of Tower Bridge, the Royal Docks were crucial to the life of the city and the nation, and for that reason they were the first target of the Luftwaffe during the Blitz. The docks were rebuilt after the war but times were already moving on. In 1981, only sixty years after the last of the Royal Docks was completed, all three were closed down and redeveloped as London City Airport, which opened in 1987 and now serves nearly three million passengers per year.

On the Isle of Dogs, just upstream of the Royal Docks, were two more extensive groups of enclosed docks: West India Docks and Millwall Docks. These, too, suffered the same fate as the Royal Docks and were closed down in 1980. The following year the Isle of Dogs was made an 'Enterprise Zone' in which developers could claim tax advantages. This coincided with a massive demand for office space in the City at a time when City planners were refusing new buildings, and with hindsight the solution seems obvious: build a new city from scratch in docklands, where land was cheaper, tax could be reclaimed, and architects could start with a blank canvas rather than being restricted by City planning regulations. In fact, at the time it was an extremely risky venture to build a new city out in the boondocks, but it has proved a success. Canary Wharf – so named because tomatoes and bananas were once landed there from the Canary Islands – is the largest office development ever to have taken place in London, providing the equivalent of one seventh

RIGHT: London and the River Thames at night, looking east from over Southwark Bridge. London Bridge is in the foreground with Tower Bridge beyond and the towers of Canary Wharf in the distance.

ABOVE: The Canary Wharf office development on the Isle of Dogs.

RIGHT AND OPPOSITE: The Royal Docks in 1935 and 2008. Royal Albert Dock, to the left, was the largest of the Royal Group of Docks while King George V Dock was the youngest, opening in 1921. Just sixty years later the entire Royal Group was closed down, and what was once the bustling centre quay now serves as the 1,200-metre runway of City Airport, which was opened by the Queen in 1987.

of all the office space in the City at the time it was begun. Canary Wharf's three landmark towers can be seen from as far afield as Kent and Essex, and include One Canada Square which, at 244 metres, is Britain's tallest building.

But Canary Wharf feels alien. It is unlike the rest of London because it is the only part of London that has been planned and built from scratch, rather than evolving organically. With no height restrictions, no historic street plan to conform to, and no worries about blocking sightlines to historic monuments, the biggest restriction on developers was cost. And the most cost-effective way of getting 55,000 office workers to their desks was a simple North American-style grid with neat, rectangular towers and an integrated transport system. Canary Wharf also had something the City had always missed – room to expand and develop further by extending the grid.

The changing use of the docks and the river is an indication of the changing nature of London itself. If the docks were the gateway to the city, the river was its industrial and commercial highway, lined with wharves as far upstream as Battersea. But today, as the docks have given way to the airport and the Canary Wharf development, so, further upstream, the river's industry and commerce have given way to residence and leisure. Warehouses and wharves have been converted into restaurants and executive flats; docks have been converted into marinas for luxury yachts or concreted over for shopping malls and exhibition centres; Bankside power station has become the Tate Modern art gallery and Battersea power station lies derelict after a failed attempt to convert it into a leisure park. The docklands and the river reflect a city where the structure of work has changed so much that the fabric of the city itself has changed to match it.

ISLE OF DOGS

The Isle of Dogs from over Greenwich, looking very faux-Manhattan. The L-shaped dock in the centre is the former Millwall Dock, now flanked by the London Arena on its right and Enterprise Business Park on its left. The green area to the east of the island is Mudchute, which was formed by the silt from the dredging of Millwall Dock. To the north, on the former West India Docks, are the corporate towers of London's biggest ever office development, Canary Wharf. Across the river to the east is the Greenwich Peninsula with the Millennium Dome (now known as O_2) at its tip.

SOUTHWARK

Rewinds

STEPNEY

GR

THE THAMES

London is an ever-changing city, yet much remains the same. Since the 1940s Luftwaffe photo was taken (previous page), new buildings have risen inexorably higher, yet the medieval street plan remains intact. London Bridge railway station was rebuilt in 1979 but the tracks make the same great diagonal scar across the centre of both pages where they are carried for four straight miles through south London on an amazing 878 brick arches. In 1929, politician John Burns described the river as 'liquid history', and while London's defining feature from the air looks little changed, its role is much altered. Once-bustling docks have been closed and the river's use has transferred from industry to leisure. Among the most recent additions is the Millennium Bridge (fourth bridge from left), which opened in 2000 as London's first new bridge since Tower Bridge (furthest right) opened in 1894. Further east, in the first loop of the river, the 300 acres of the Surrey Commercial Docks have been almost entirely filled in; they were redeveloped in the 1980s with a retail park, leisure park and more than 6,000 homes. On the Isle of Dogs (far right), 90 acres of docks have been redeveloped as office blocks which include Britain's tallest building. Between Tower Bridge and London Bridge is HMS *Belfast*, which was still on active service when the earlier photograph was taken. Its guns have a range of over 14 miles, so it could bombard Heston Services on the M4 or Scratchwood on the M1 from its current permanent mooring.

RHONDDA VALLEY

In 1860 the green and peaceful valleys of the River Rhondda in South Wales were home to farming communities totalling less than 3,000 people. Just fifty years later, in 1910, the Rhondda was the engine room of British industry – black and smoky, and with a population of more than 160,000. The Rhondda was still an industrial powerhouse in 1940, when the archive picture was taken, but the coal mining industry went into perpetual decline after the Second World War and today its population has shrunk to some 60,000. The smoke and the winding gear are distant memories, while the spoil heaps – which dominate both the foreground and the horizon of the older picture – have grassed over to look like ancient barrows or hill forts.

In the eighteenth century, coal enabled Britain to become the first country in the world to industrialise. The skies of northern England blackened, but still the Rhondda remained idyllic and peaceful. In the mid-nineteenth century,

however, coal was discovered in South Wales and the valleys were transformed. Britain's hunger for coal was at its height, and the Welsh valleys provided the perfect landscape to meet this need. The long, steep-sided ribbons of land made it relatively easy to extract the coal, and migrant workers flooded into the Rhondda creating mining towns in an area that had known only isolated farmsteads. But the boom was to be limited. The post-war decline in the local industry hit the Rhondda harder than many other mining communities. There was no other industry for the local population to turn to and the land remained scarred and abandoned.

However, as the valleys return from black to green a new industry is emerging. Tourism is now one of Wales's biggest industries, with overseas and domestic tourists spending some £3 billion a year on trips to the principality – an average of more than £8 million every day.

CARDIFF BAY

During the 1990s, Cardiff Bay was transformed from a vast expanse of redundant docklands into a thriving waterfront development by a tidal barrage built across the mouth of the bay from Queen Alexandra Dock to Penarth Head. These photographs show views in opposite directions across the bay, with Queen Alexandra Dock to the right of the 1960s image and to the left of the modern one.

The bay's origins as a port date from 1839 when the second Marquis of Bute built a dock on the Taff estuary close to Cardiff, which was then a small town of some 2,000 inhabitants. The Marquis soon opened several more docks, and in feathering the family nest by ensuring that all the coal and iron produced on the family land was exported via the family docks, the Butes also ensured the future of Cardiff itself – by the turn of the twentieth century the population had increased to 182,000 and Cardiff was one of the world's busiest ports, exporting more than 10 million tons of coal a year.

Cardiff was made capital of Wales in 1955 but the last deal in the city's famous Coal Exchange was struck just three years later, and by the 1960s, when the earlier photograph was taken, the docks and the surrounding industry were in decline. Regeneration of the docks was problematic because of the huge 14-metre tidal range (the second largest in the world) which left the bay inaccessible for up to fourteen hours

of every twenty-four. The answer was the Cardiff Bay Barrage, which was built from 1994-99 to create a 500-acre non-tidal freshwater lake with eight miles of waterfront which has been redeveloped with shops, restaurants, hotels, visitor attractions and landmark buildings, such as the Wales Millennium Centre (the bronze-roofed building near the centre of the modern picture) and, to its left, the National Assembly for Wales.

GLASGOW DOCKS

By 1901 Glasgow was known as 'The Second City of the Empire'. The city's rise was the result of the Industrial Revolution and Glasgow's pre-eminence as a port, which saw the construction of extensive enclosed docks such as Queen's Dock, on the near side of the River Clyde in both photographs, and Prince's Dock on the far side. Both were built in the late nineteenth century at the height of the Victorian era (they were named after Queen Victoria and her consort Prince Albert). By 1966, however, when the earlier photograph was taken, the docks were in severe decline – they were closed just three years later, and all bar the square inlet of West Quay (to the right of both pictures) was filled in and concreted over. Surviving landmarks include the two rotundas, one on each side of the Clyde to the left of both pictures, which housed hydraulic lifts giving access to the Harbour Tunnel. The tunnel was completed in

1896 and remained in use for traffic until 1943 and for pedestrians until 1980. The crane that appears in both pictures is known as the Finnieston Crane but should technically be called the Stobcross Crane, which is where it now resides. The original, which stood 450 metres further west at Finnieston, was removed to make way for a bridge which was never built. It was replaced in 1932 with the present 175-ton electric crane, which stands 59 metres high and was used for loading railway locomotives and other machinery onto cargo ships.

The Finnieston Crane has been dubbed Glasgow's Eiffel Tower, and today it stands close to another Glasgow icon, 'The Armadillo'. Properly known as the Clyde Auditorium, this 3,000-seat venue was designed by Sir Norman Foster and opened in 1997 as a spectacular addition to the adjacent Scottish Exhibition and Conference Centre.

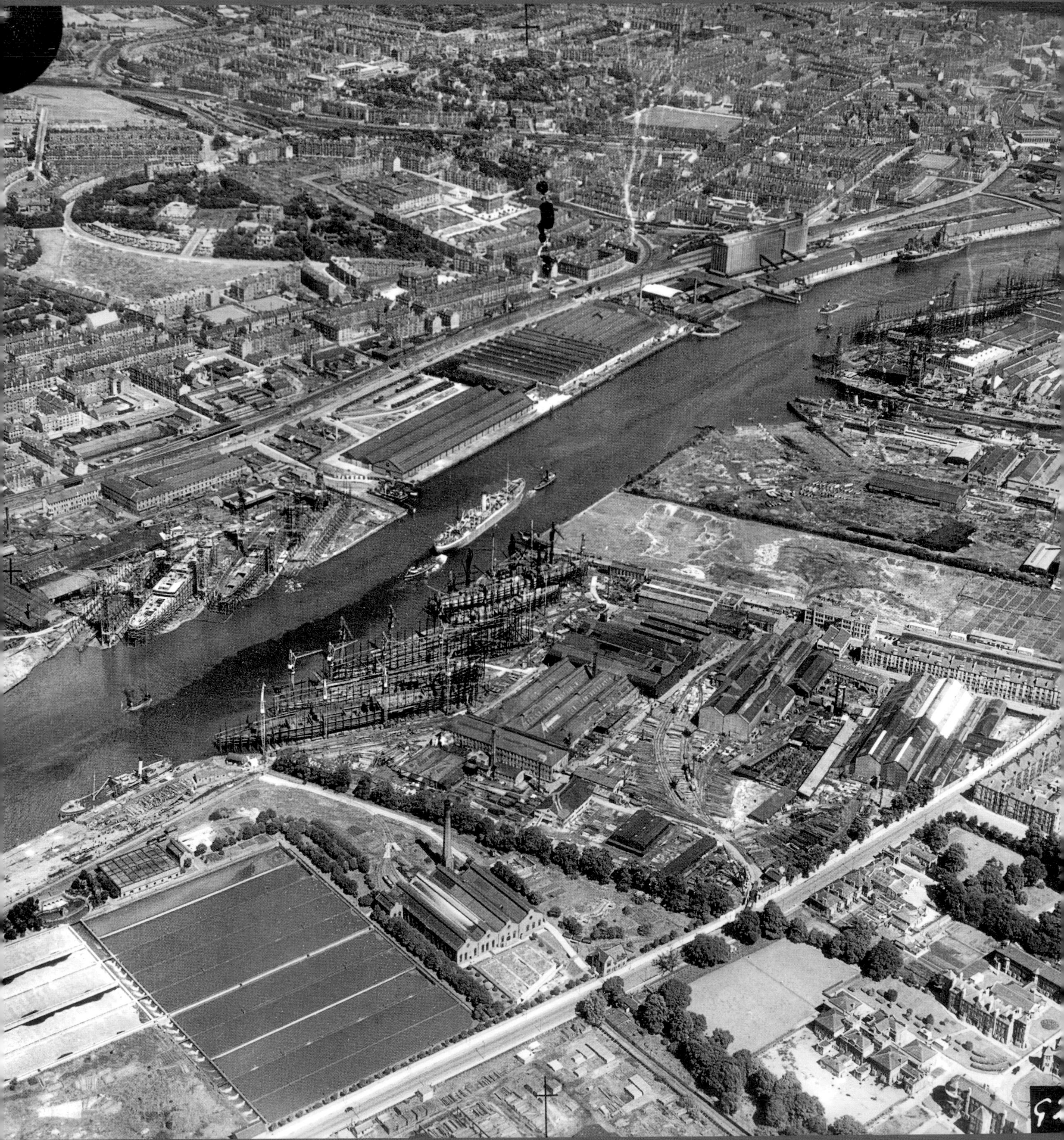

CLYDE SHIPYARDS

By the late nineteenth century, Glasgow's River Clyde was synonymous with shipbuilding. In 1850 Clyde shipyards produced 20,000 tons of shipping; by 1900 that had more than doubled to 50,000 tons, and by the First World War the Clyde was producing 800,000 tons of shipping every year and employing more than 100,000 workers. But it didn't last. Recession hit Glasgow between the wars, and after the Second World War shipbuilding declined for good – during the 60s countless shipyards closed and the Clyde became an industrial wasteland.

The 1940 photograph shows Barclay Curle & Co's Clydeholme Shipyard to the left of the picture on the far bank of the Clyde; Alexander Stephen & Sons' Linthouse Shipyard opposite Clydeholme; and Fairfield Shipyard on the near bank to the right of the picture.

Barclay Curle & Co moved to Clydeholme in 1855 to build bigger vessels, and in 1911 the firm built *Jutlandia*, the first ocean-going diesel

vessel to be built in Britain. Later sold to Tyneside shipbuilders Swan Hunter, the yard closed in 1965. In 1869 Alexander Stephen bought the Linthouse Estate, opposite Clydeholme, and converted 20 acres of it into a shipyard and workshops. From 1904-49 Stephen & Sons built banana boats for Elders & Fyffes, and during the Second World War the yard built and repaired scores of vessels for the Royal Navy; it closed in 1968.

The Fairfield Shipyard was laid out in 1864 and soon became one of the most important in Europe. Some of the fastest ships of the time were built here – including several winners of the Blue Riband for the fastest time between Britain and New York – and during the Second World War the yard built thirty naval vessels including HMS *Howe*. The yard is currently known as Govan Shipyard and is owned by BAe Marine, which is building several Type 45 destroyers here for the Royal Navy.

RAVENSCRAIG STEEL

By the Second World War, one private company controlled more than 80 per cent of Scotland's steel production – Colvilles Ltd. After the war Colvilles began a massive programme of expansion and modernisation which included building Ravenscraig, a new integrated iron and steelworks on 1,125 acres of green fields near Motherwell, to the south-east of Glasgow. Work began in 1953, the ovens and furnaces were first lit in 1957, and the construction of a new strip mill – one of only four in the UK – meant that by 1962 Ravenscraig looked much as it does in the picture on the left taken in the late 1970s.

Colvilles was nationalised in 1967 and Ravenscraig struggled through the 1970s as part of the British Steel Corporation (BSC). It was narrowly saved from closure in the early 1980s by political pressure and lobbying to prevent the massive unemployment that would result,

but when BSC was privatised in 1988 the writing was on the wall. The strip mill was decommissioned in April 1991, and in September 1992 the entire plant was shut down with the direct loss of 1,200 jobs.

Ravenscraig consumed so much energy it had its own power station. The cooling towers are lost in the haze of the earlier photograph but their position is revealed by the white plume of steam rising at the centre of the picture. They were demolished in 1996 along with the gas-holder bearing the famous name of Ravenscraig, and the rest of the site has since been flattened. The fields are turning green again, but perhaps not for long. Ambitious twenty-year regeneration proposals include the development of thousands of new homes, dedicated business and industrial areas, education and skills centres, retail centres and a new railway station.

AYR HOLIDAY CAMP

Daniel Defoe, the author of *Robinson Crusoe*, described Ayr as being 'like an old Beauty, shewing the Ruins of a good Face.' He wrote that the town was 'not only decay'd and declin'd but decaying and declining every Day', and that 'nothing will save it from Death if Trade does not revive.' But he wasn't counting on the fame Ayr would earn from its association with Robbie Burns, who was born in the neighbouring village – now suburb – of Alloway, or the effect of the

railways. It wasn't trade, but tourism that saved Ayr. Thanks to the opening of the Glasgow-Ayr railway in 1840 the town became a popular Victorian holiday resort, famous for its long sandy beaches, its race course and its golf courses.

Today Ayr remains a popular holiday resort, but the Craig Tara holiday camp to the north of the town owes its existence not to the railway but to yet another twist of fate. At the start of the

Second World War the government requisitioned several Butlins holiday camps for use as military bases, and commissioned Billy Butlin to build another one on the south coast of England. But after the fall of France the south coast was deemed too dangerous, so Butlin was asked instead to build camps in Pwllheli in Wales and Ayr in Scotland. The Ayr camp opened in 1941 as Navy training camp HMS *Scotia*, and after the war it was transferred to Butlins and reopened in 1947 as a holiday camp with Scottish variations on the traditional Butlins theme – for instance, the Redcoats wore kilts and campers were woken by live pipers rather than piped music from Radio Butlin.

The camp even had its own railway station to receive holidaymakers direct from Glasgow,

Newcastle and Leeds but the line closed in 1968 shortly after the earlier picture (left) was taken. In 1987, Butlins announced a £25 million investment in the camp. Improvements included an indoor water complex known as 'Wondersplash', a new 900-seat food court, the remodelling of the caravan park and a vast expansion in the amount and standard of accommodation. In 1999 the camp was transferred to Butlins' sister company Haven Holidays and another £12.5 million development plan was announced. This included demolishing many of the camp buildings and replacing most of the chalets with luxury caravans (above). The camp was officially reopened as Craig Tara in 1999 by Scottish football legend Kenny Dalglish.

MEADOWHALL STEEL

Sheffield was built on iron and steel. Iron smelting was its main industry from as early as the twelfth century, and by the fourteenth century this South Yorkshire city had built up a reputation for fine cutlery and silverware that lasts to this day. Even before the Industrial Revolution the novelist, adventurer and travel writer Daniel Defoe wrote of Sheffield's 'houses dark and black, occasioned by the continued smoke of forges, which are always at work.' And when the Industrial Revolution did arrive,

Sheffield remained at the fore. By the Second World War the city's iron and steel was so important to the war effort that Sheffield was heavily bombed by the Luftwaffe. In the post-war period, however, the steel industry steadily declined, hitting the city hard and leading to the closure of many industrial sites during the 1980s.

During the 1990s Sheffield's steel industry enjoyed a partial revival, and the city now produces alloys, special steel, cutlery, magnets

and precision tools, but many industrial sites have been redeveloped. One such site is the Meadowhall Steelworks, photographed in 1951 (left) and as it is today (right). Meadowhall Road and the River Don are proof that both photographs show the same place but the only surviving evidence of the steelworks is the twin cooling towers at the top of both pictures – and even they are the subject of a local conservation campaign to save them from demolition.

An elevated section of the M1 motorway cuts across the top of the modern picture, isolating the cooling towers from the site they once served – a site which has been transformed from a twentieth-century version of the black and smoky industry described by Defoe into a bright temple of commerce and modernity. Opened in 1990, the Meadowhall shopping centre has nearly 1.4 million square feet of retail space and more than 270 shops and restaurants. It is one of Europe's most successful shopping centres, serving some 30 million visitors each year and thus living up to its billing as 'The Land of Shoppertunity'.

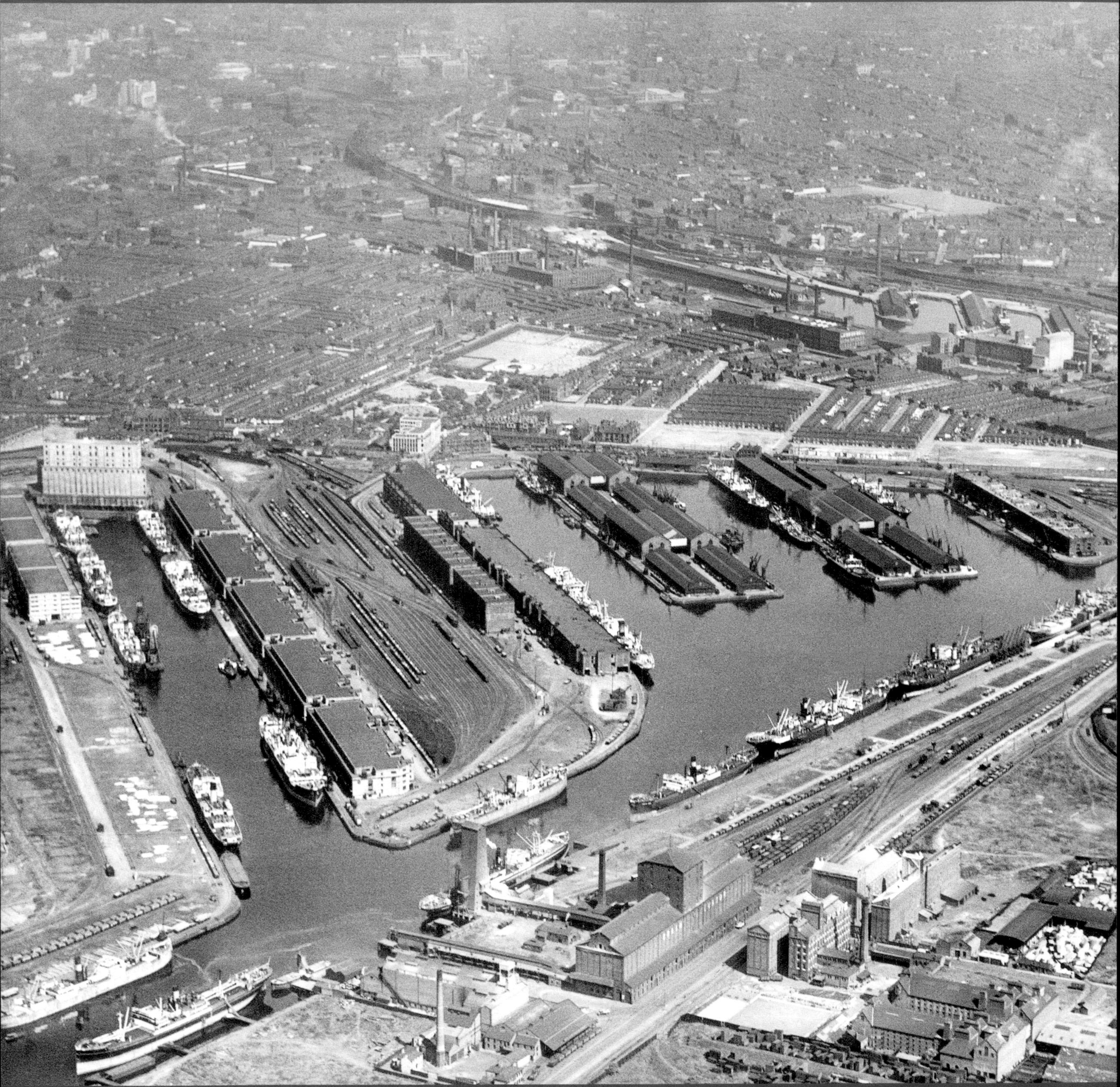

MANCHESTER SHIP CANAL

The 'Canal Age' began in Manchester with the world's first wholly manmade waterway, the Bridgewater Canal. Canals may seem quaint now but before the advent of our road and rail network they were vital to Britain's industry, and the Duke of Bridgewater's pioneering spirit in building a canal to transport coal from his estates is commemorated on his gravestone: 'he sent barges across fields the farmers formerly tilled.'

The Bridgewater Canal was completed in 1767 and it sparked a craze for canal-building which meant that by 1830 Britain had an amazing network of 4,000 miles of navigable inland waterways. Very few new canals were built after that date, with one notable exception – the Manchester Ship Canal, which was cut from 1887-94 with the aim of attracting trade to Manchester from the docks at Liverpool. The investment worked, and despite being 36 miles inland, Manchester soon became Britain's third

busiest port. The docks completely transformed Salford, at the top of both pictures, and Trafford Park, at the bottom. Trafford Park had been a deer park but over the next decade it developed into the world's first planned industrial estate, employing over 75,000 workers.

The docks were still busy in 1933, when the archive picture was taken, but with the decline of heavy industry the importance of the canal has diminished. It now handles a fraction of its former tonnage and ships now dock further from the city centre. Salford Docks were closed in 1982 and redeveloped as Salford Quays, which includes high-rise residential towers and the landmark Lowry Arts Centre on the waterside. The Lowry Footbridge links Salford Quays to Trafford Park, which has also been redeveloped with its own landmark building, architect Daniel Liebskind's Imperial War Museum North (bottom centre).

WATFORD GAP

Watford Gap has two claims to fame: one as Britain's first motorway service station and another as the traditional frontier post delineating the nation's north-south divide. The phrase 'north of the Watford Gap' can be a term of disparagement or pride, depending on one's perspective.

The name of this M1 service station in Nottinghamshire is a matter of mystery to those who wonder why it is named after the town in Hertfordshire. It is actually named after a break in the hills close to the tiny village of Watford; the village lies just out of frame to the right, served by the bridge that crosses the motorway

to the top left of both photographs. The Watford Gap has facilitated north-south transport since the Romans routed Watling Street through it almost 2,000 years ago. Today, several routes run within a quarter of a mile of each other as they squeeze through the gap in the hills: the Grand Union Canal, the A5, the M1 motorway and the West Coast railway line, which is just visible in the bottom left of both pictures.

Watford Gap only just made it into the history books as Britain's first service station – it opened on 2 November 1959, the same day as the M1 motorway, but the catering facilities weren't ready and the operator, Blue Boar, had to sell sandwiches from hastily erected garden sheds. The cafés didn't open until September 1960, the year before this photograph was taken, by which time the Fortes services at Newport Pagnell were fully open, giving Newport Pagnell a rival claim to being Britain's first service station. The initial plan was to reserve Newport Pagnell for cars and Watford Gap for lorries but this was never implemented, hence the mix of vehicles using the services in both pictures. At first the concept of service stations and motorways was so novel that there was even a television programme explaining how to leave the motorway and use the service area. By the end of the 1960s, however, there were sixteen service stations in operation and eleven more under construction. The Ministry of Transport stipulated that service areas should be double-sided, a requirement which was met at Watford Gap by having rotationally symmetrical sites linked by a new footbridge. The footbridge appears in both photographs but the symmetry of the sites has been lost as the facilities have expanded. The rise of the motorways coincided with a rise in touring rock bands, as a result of which Watford Gap – or 'the Blue Boar', as it was often known – has passed into urban legend. Gerry Marsden of Gerry and the Pacemakers described it as good for 'a quick stop and a quick nosh' and often ran into other bands there, but Roy Harper was less impressed – his song 'Watford Gap' was so disparaging that owners Blue Boar succeeded in forcing him to drop it from future UK copies of his album *Bullinamingvase*. Legend has it that the services were so famous among musicians that when Jimi Hendrix first visited Britain he thought Blue Boar was the name of a nightclub.

CAMBRIDGE SCIENCE PARK

The land to the left of the archive picture and the centre of the modern one has belonged to Trinity College, Cambridge, since the College was founded by Henry VIII in 1546. Since then the rural farmland has seen several major changes including the arrival of the railway in the nineteenth century, which cuts across the top of the archive picture, and the encroachment of terraced houses for the Cambridge suburb of Chesterton.

In 1942 the land was requisitioned by the US Army, which constructed the geometric patterns of buildings to the bottom left of the 1952 picture as a base to prepare tanks and other vehicles for D-Day. After the war the site was abandoned for twenty-five years until Trinity College decided to develop the land as Britain's first science park.

The development of the science park in the 1960s was a response to a Labour government initiative aimed at boosting Britain's technological development. The government encouraged universities and industry to co-operate by sharing their expertise, research and investment, so Cambridge University began looking for ways to stimulate the expansion of science-based industry near Cambridge. During the 1950s Stanford University had established the world's first science park in California, and in 1971 Trinity College decided to follow suit by developing its derelict brownfield site. Two years later Laser-Scan became the first company to move into Cambridge Science Park, which is now home to more than ninety technology-led companies.

HAPPISBURGH, NORFOLK

At first glance it looks like the same scene: the caravan park, the sleepy village, the lighthouse set absurdly far back from the cliff. But a closer look reveals the astonishing rate at which this part of the British coastline is being eroded. In the 1995 picture (left) there are five rows of caravans between the site track and the cliff edge; in the later one there are just four rows. Further along the coast the sea defences have been reduced to tatters and the concrete slope known as the Town Gap ramp has disappeared altogether. This slope was the Happisburgh lifeboat launch ramp but it collapsed in 2002 and the lifeboat has been re-stationed further down the coast. The following year a 30-metre stretch of cliff collapsed, taking with it a number of properties together with the road that served them. And on the extreme left of the pictures the road that once served houses standing well back from the cliff edge now leads straight into a new bay that the sea has bitten out of the coast.

The sea has encroached by tens of metres in just thirteen years due to a combination of wind, waves, rising sea levels, and 'tectonic tilt'. When the ice retreated after the last Ice Age the reduced weight on some parts of the landscape resulted in a seesaw effect which is still causing some parts of the land to rise and others to sink at a rate of up to 1.5 cm per decade. The traditional answer has been to build hard sea defences but this is costly, ultimately ineffective, and has a knock-on effect of increasing erosion on other parts of the coast. For this reason a government quango has recently concluded that the best solution is to allow nine miles of sea defences along the Norfolk coast to collapse.

HEATHROW AIRPORT

In 1929 aviation pioneer Richard Fairey built a small aerodrome on Hounslow Heath, close to the village of Heath Row. Fairey assured local residents that because it was a test aerodrome there would be few flights, but during the Second World War aviation minister Harold Balfour used emergency powers to compulsorily purchase Fairey's aerodrome and the land around it.

The village of Heath Row was demolished to make way for Heathrow Airport, which opened to civilians on 31 May 1946. There was one runway and few facilities other than a row of huts but work progressed quickly, and by the time the older photograph was taken in 1954 there were three pairs of runways, a control tower in the middle of the central island, and a terminal building known as the Europa Building. The present Terminal 1 opened in 1969 to the top right of the central island, the Europa Building

became Terminal Two, and what had been an annexe for domestic flights, to the bottom left of the central island, became Terminal Three.

During the 1970s, main runways were lengthened from 2,740 to 3,660 and 3,900 metres and still Heathrow continued to expand. Prince Charles opened Terminal 4 in 1986 (bottom right of the modern picture) and the Queen opened Terminal 5 in 2008, to the left of the modern picture between the main runways. The last of Heathrow's original four shorter runways was decommissioned in 2005, leading to pressure from the aviation lobby for a third main runway. Even before the opening of T5, Heathrow was the world's busiest airport in terms of international passengers, used by over ninety airlines carrying more than 67 million passengers a year to some 170 destinations. When T5 is fully operational, passenger numbers are expected to rise to more than 100 million per year.

CITY OF LONDON

The City of London is a city within a city. What
we now know as Greater London originated here,
and although the original City long ago outgrew
its city walls, it remains a separate entity from
the rest of London with its own police force, its
own unique customs, and a maze-like street
plan dating back to the Middle Ages. This
densely packed web of streets is clearly visible
in the 1935 picture and still exists in the modern

one, though it is obscured by the proliferation
of mid- and high-rise buildings.

The most dramatic change is the cluster
of landmark towers to the left of the modern
picture. The tallest among them are the sleek,
dark glass of Tower 42 and the curved profile of
30 St Mary Axe, better known as 'The Gherkin'.
The towers are a modern testament to London's
pre-eminence as a world centre of finance and

insurance, but that pre-eminence dates back long before the advent of skyscrapers. Tower 42 was built close to where Elizabeth I's financial adviser, Thomas Gresham lived; Lloyd's of London, the world's largest insurance market, originated in a seventeenth-century coffee house run by Edward Lloyd; and the Bank of England has stood on Threadneedle Street since moving there in 1734, forty years after its incorporation by William III to finance war against France. The Bank is more prominent in the older picture,

standing upper right at the focal point of the six major streets that converge just below the imposing roof of Cannon Street Station. The station is all but invisible in the modern picture. Together with Liverpool Street Station (bottom left) Cannon Street helps the City cope with the most widely fluctuating population of any city in the world – with only 9,000 permanent residents, the population increases forty-fold every weekday as more than a third of a million commuters arrive for work.

THE ISLE OF DOGS

There are various theories as to the origin of the name 'Isle of Dogs'. One is based on a tragic legend about a nobleman and his bride celebrating their wedding by hunting there but drowning in the marshes, after which the hunting dogs began howling for their master. Another is that the royal hunting pack was kennelled there when past monarchs visited Greenwich Palace, and a third is that the name derives from the Flemish dijk (dyke), referring to the embankments that once protected the marshland from flooding. Although this area has been known as the Isle of Dogs for centuries it did not become an island until 1805 when a canal was cut across the neck of the peninsula to save ships travelling three miles round the loop of the river.

By the end of the eighteenth century the river was so busy that merchants realised London could only continue functioning as a port if enclosed docks were built. The first of those docks were the West India Docks, visible at the bottom left of the 1934 picture. These were built from 1800 1802, enclosing 54 acres and served by three quarters of a mile of warehouses. The 36-acre L-shaped Millwall Dock, at the centre of the older picture, followed in 1868. The name Millwall refers to a line of windmills that once stood on the embankment to drain the marshland, and it gave its name to a football team founded by workers at Morton's jam factory – the club kept the name even after moving south of the river in 1910. London's importance as a port declined and the docks closed in 1980,

since when an explosion of office development has transformed West India Docks. The development centres on Canary Wharf – so named because tomatoes and bananas were once landed there from the Canary Islands – whose main tower, officially known as One Canada Square, is Britain's tallest building at 244 metres.

The great migration

Every twenty-four hours, five times a week, Britain is shaken by a momentous event that would be considered an amazing phenomenon if it didn't happen so regularly. Each morning some 48 million Britons – almost 80 per cent of the entire population – join a nationwide migration of people travelling from their homes to work, to school, or some other destination. For many people, travelling between, into, or across Britain's cities during the three hours of 'rush hour' feels like unfettered chaos, but viewing this daily mass movement of people from above reveals that there is some semblance of organisation behind the disarray.

The vast majority of people travel to work or school by road, mostly in their car or on one of the UK's 76,000 buses. But the idea of living in one place and commuting to and from work in another pre-dates the car: it began with the arrival of the railways and the consequent building of the suburbs in the mid-nineteenth century. More than 175 years later, some three million people cram themselves aboard the trains of Britain's aged railways every morning. Ours is the oldest rail network in the world and one of the most overworked – for instance, the railways of Kent carry more trains than the entire rail system of Switzerland. Britain's railways are a constant source of complaint from commuters about packed trains, cancellations and delays, and the root causes can be found in the history and geography of the rail network.

The first railway in the world to carry fare-paying passengers was the Oystermouth Railway in Wales, in 1804, but that used horse-drawn wagons. More famously, George Stephenson's Stockton & Darlington Railway opened in 1825 as the first steam railway to carry passengers as well as freight, followed five years later by the world's first intercity railway, the Liverpool & Manchester. Then the network began to expand. When lines were first built the tracks wound through open countryside but now many of them are hemmed in by row upon row of suburban streets – streets which were only built because of the existence of the

railway. But these streets leave no room for growth, so in many areas a single pair of tracks now has to carry up to ten times more passengers a day than was designed for. In these areas there is also no room for fast trains to overtake slow ones or for 'lane closures', so a single delayed or broken-down train, cracked rail or signal failure can bring an entire line grinding to a halt.

In addition to the problems of capacity, there is also the problem of routing. When the network was first built some lines could not be built on the most direct route because Victorian landowners refused to sell their land, so the railways had to be routed round the great estates. Ironically James Watt, the son of the great steam engine pioneer, was one of these Victorian NIMBYs – because he refused to sell

part of his estate in Aston, near Birmingham, and for many years the lines from London to Birmingham could not be linked with the lines from Birmingham to Manchester and Liverpool.

RIGHT: Edinburgh's Waverley Station, which opened in 1846, is named after Sir Walter Scott's novel *Waverley*. It was remodelled from 1892 to 1902 when it took on its present plan of two termini back to back, with twenty-one platforms and an area of 23 acres, making it Britain's largest passenger station by area at the time – it is currently the second largest, after London Waterloo, and handles more than 16 million passengers a year, or nearly 44,000 every day.

BELOW: London's Liverpool Street Station at night. The poet John Betjeman described it as 'the most picturesque and interesting of the London termini' but the two-part layout was impractical so it was remodelled between 1985 and 1991 and now serves nearly 57 million passengers a year, or more than 156,000 per day.

Another factor affecting routing is geography. It is very easy to travel up and down the UK by rail but far harder to travel across the country because the Pennines stretch more than half the length of England, from Birmingham to Scotland – and trains can't climb steep hills. Consequently there is just one line crossing the Pennines from east to west, and it is one of the slowest lines in the country. This restriction means that it is pointless making certain journeys by rail: for instance, Newcastle to Manchester – a distance of 100 miles as the crow flies – is 180 miles by rail, and Sheffield to Stoke-on-Trent – 34 miles as the crow flies – is nearly 100 miles by rail.

But, despite all these problems, people continue using the rail network in their millions. Over the last decade there has been a 40 per cent increase in the number of rail journeys, and Britons now make more than a billion journeys a year by train – as many as in 1946, when very few people owned cars. And one of the reasons for that is that Britain's road network is just as overcrowded as its rail network.

CHAOS ON OUR ROADS

The average UK commuter travels the equivalent of two and a half times round the world in the course of his or her working life. But commuting originally meant something entirely different – it meant exchanging one form of obligation for another. It was nineteenth-century Americans who started using the word to mean travelling regularly to and from work; the commutation, or exchange, was the payment in advance for journeys on public transport. So to begin with the only true commuters were holders of railway season tickets. The first travellers in Britain to be known as commuters were passengers on the Liverpool & Manchester railway, which first sold 'commutation tickets' in 1842, but since then the word has come to mean anyone who travels regularly to and from work, even if it is by car. Ironically the millions of people who commute by car every day in Britain are putting our road network under even more pressure than the rail commuters do our aged rail network.

Every day more than 12 million vehicles plough into Britain's cities in a grinding stop-start of frustration that pollutes the atmosphere and raises drivers' stress levels. The problem starts on the motorways and trunk roads leading into the cities, but traffic chaos on these major roads is not a problem that can be solved by building more roads. Studies carried out in the 1990s showed that building more roads simply encourages more journeys and the level of congestion remains fairly constant. But congestion on trunk roads is nothing compared with the traffic chaos that ensues when all those cars reach our city centres, many of which were laid out during the Middle Ages to accommodate slow-moving horse-drawn carriages and carts. In the case of London, average traffic speeds haven't improved much since the days of the horse and cart: the average speed of traffic in London was the same in 2000 as it had been in 1900 – a mere 12 mph, making it the slowest city in Europe.

Traffic planners use a range of tools to try to ease congestion in city centres, where gridlock can occur in minutes due to the knock-on effect of a single broken down car or mis-parked van, or a burst water main or a hole in the road. The most obvious tools are traffic lights, bus lanes

and parking restrictions. In London, police can alter the timing of some two-thirds of the capital's traffic lights in order to control traffic flow in response to accidents and congestion, often 'storing' blocks of traffic on long, straight roads such as Park Lane and the Marylebone Road to give traffic elsewhere time to clear. At other times, traffic is allowed to flow along these routes and London taxi drivers talk about 'riding the green wave' on those rare occasions when the lights on the Marylebone Road all change at the right moment.

There are also less obvious 'secret weapons' to control congestion. Traffic planners have started closing roads or restricting their use, having found that reducing the number of roads in use eases the flow of traffic because there are fewer junctions to negotiate. The subtlest trick of all is not to close a road but to alter its appearance by repaving streets in warm stone, getting rid of the kerbstones and changing the colour of the tarmac. This makes certain roads feel 'pedestrianised' and many drivers avoid using them. However, the effectiveness of this ploy is limited because ultimately closing roads reduces capacity. The only real way to combat rising road congestion is to change people's commuting habits. The Commission for Integrated Transport has calculated that congestion could be cut by 40 per cent without altering the current road network if people were prepared to accept radical social changes such as rationing road use, car-sharing, encouraging more children to walk to school and staggering work patterns to allow people to start at different times. But acceptance is unlikely because just as 'an Englishman's home is his castle', for many Britons their car is the trusty steed on which they venture forth into the world beyond.

From above, the most dramatic change to Britain's landscape in the last sixty years has been the appearance of the motorways. The country's first motorway was the 8-mile Preston by-pass, which was opened by Prime Minister Harold Macmillan in December 1958 and now forms part of the M6. This short section was a sign of things to come – eleven months later,

transport minister Ernest Marples opened Britain's first major motorway, a 75-mile section of the M1, saying: 'This motorway starts a new era in road travel. It is in keeping with the bold, exciting and scientific era in which we live.' For better or worse, Marples was right that it was the start of a new era – the 1960s and 70s were the golden age of motorway building, and by 1984 the network extended to 1,731 miles. Since then, for environmental and financial reasons, motorway building has slowed down, with just over 470 miles built during the next quarter of a century, bringing the total length of Britain's current motorway network to 2,201.88 miles.

One of the symptoms of the weight of traffic is a unique feature of motorways: the phantom traffic jam. Suddenly, all three lanes will grind to a halt for no apparent reason. Seen from above, the answer becomes obvious – one driver brakes too harshly and if the person behind is driving too close they brake even harder, starting a chain reaction of braking that brings the traffic further back to a standstill. So if people drove less aggressively, and kept a greater distance from the car in front, phantom traffic jams would occur much

BELOW: Computer-generated image showing the movement of thousands of London taxis, mapped second by second as they move round the city. The brightest areas are the most frequented routes, the brightest of all being Hyde Park Corner at the southern end of Park Lane.

BOTTOM: Trucks queueing on the A20 as they head towards the docks at Dover. The Port of Dover is one of Britain's busiest ferry ports, handling 14.3 million passengers, 2.8 million cars and more than 105,000 coaches in 2007. It is also Britain's fourth busiest cargo port in terms of tonnage handled, mainly roll-on roll-off freight on lorries like the ones queueing here. In 2007 Dover handled 2,363,583 road haulage vehicles – an average of 6,475 per day, which explains the congestion on the A20.

less often. To make matters worse, phantom traffic jams don't just affect vehicles in the immediate vicinity – because traffic can't pull away at the same rate it slowed down and stopped, the concertina effect ripples back down the motorway at its own steady speed of 10 miles an hour, and won't disappear until it runs out of road or the density of the traffic falls below a critical level.

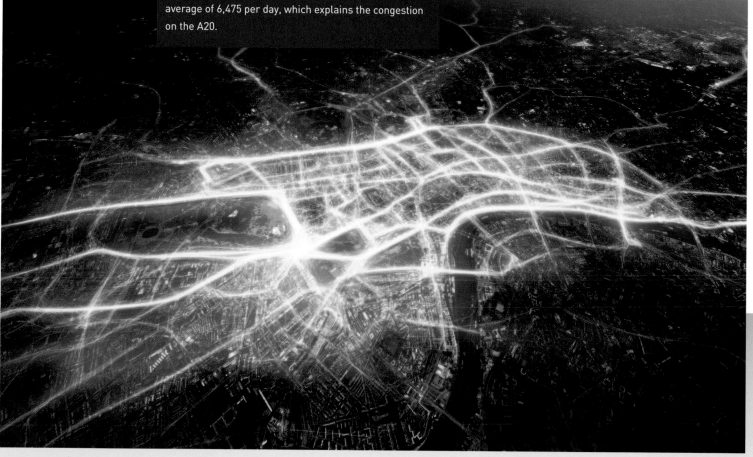

MOTORWAY MADNESS

Looking south-east across the M25/M11 interchange, north of London, at night. There is a saying that all roads in England lead to London and all roads in London lead to the centre, but that is not true of the M25, which goes round the capital in a 117-mile distorted circle. Work started on the first sections of the M25 in 1973 and various sections opened in stages from 1975 until 1986, when the completed orbital motorway was officially opened by Prime Minister Margaret Thatcher. The M25 accounts for just over 5 per cent of Britain's motorway network but carries more than 15 per cent of motorway traffic, leading to such bad traffic congestion that it is often referred to as the world's most expensive car park.

AERIAL TRAFFIC JAMS

Britain's rush hour is not confined to our roads, railways and motorways – there is also a hidden motorway network above our heads with its own clearly demarcated routes, junctions, forbidden areas and holding patterns – and even its own aerial motorway cops. In the last ten years there have been an average of 3.9 million commercial aircraft movements at British airports every year – an average of nearly 11,000 take-offs and landings every day. Every morning, hundreds of these aircraft converge on Britain's airports from all over the world, all looking for space on the rush-hour runways to land and unload their passengers.

Aircraft pass in both directions over the Scottish Borders, heading south towards Heathrow and Gatwick airports or north towards the Arctic, where they circle the globe at its narrowest latitudes and then head south again towards their destinations. Just like the trains and cars heading into London, the planes heading south hit congestion as they reach the capital. They are held in stacks like vertical queues at aerial traffic lights, flying in a spiral holding pattern until it is their turn to land. Then they are cleared for their final approach to their destination airport, which is the crunch point of the early morning aerial rush hour – each jet is only 90 seconds apart and moving at more than 200 mph. Like our roads and railways, our air traffic is often operating at the limits of tolerance, but with far greater potential consequences if pilots or air traffic controllers make an error.

ABOVE: Computer-generated image showing traces of some of the 11,000 aircraft that pass through British airspace each day, revealing just how crowded our skies are. The traces show three distinct bright patches where aircraft are stacked for Britain's three busiest airports, Heathrow, Gatwick and Stansted.

LEFT: The world's largest passenger plane, the A380 Airbus, aka the 'Superjumbo'. Capable of carrying up to 853 people, the A380 is a double-decker wide-bodied airliner with one and a half times the cabin floorspace of the next biggest airliner, the Boeing 747-400 'Jumbo Jet'. The A380 made its maiden flight in April 2005 and first went into service, with Singapore Airlines, on 25 October 2007.

STANSTED AIRPORT

Stansted Airport from the south-west. Stansted opened
in 1943 as a US Army Air Force base and in the mid-1950s
the Americans built the 3,048-metre runway that would
make it so attractive as an international airport. In the
1960s, after the Ministry of Aviation took control, Stansted
developed freight and charter holiday operations, but it
was in the 1980s, with Heathrow and Gatwick running ever
closer to capacity, that its development as London's third
airport began. Stansted is now Britain's third largest
airport, handling nearly 24 million passengers per year,
and plans have been submitted for a second runway and
terminal building.

TYPHOON IN THE LAKE DISTRICT

The skies above Britain may be crowded but civilian air traffic is restricted to certain carefully delineated air corridors (see previous page). Elsewhere, our skies are often used for training military pilots and testing aircraft such as the world's most advanced fighter, the Typhoon, better known as the Eurofighter. The Eurofighter is tested out of Warton Airfield in Lancashire, from where it is flown at altitudes ranging from just above ground level to 55,000 feet over the Irish Sea and the Lake District. The terrain of the Lake District provides an ideal training ground for flying in the narrow valleys of Helmand Province in Afghanistan, where the Eurofighter is due to be deployed in 2008.

RUSH HOUR

In addition to planes, trains and automobiles there is another element to Britain's great daily migration – pedestrians. Millions of people are lucky enough to be able to make their entire journey to work or school on foot, and millions more will walk as part of their journey. When moving en masse, groups of humans flock, migrate and move like herds of wild animals, following patterns that only become apparent from above. And just like the motorised traffic of the great migration, there are ways of measuring, analysing and managing the movement of people on foot.

To manage and protect rush-hour pedestrians in crowded cities one of the first decisions planners must make is whether to give priority to pedestrians or drivers. This may apply to the siting of crossings, the phasing of lights, the provision of bus stops and rail stations for composite journeys, or even the closing of streets to motor traffic. Another way of favouring pedestrians is, paradoxically, to have them share paved areas with cyclists. The logic is that if cyclists are given a dedicated area they will cycle faster and present a greater potential danger to any pedestrians who wander into their path, but if the two are brought together then the cyclists are forced to slow down to the speed of the pedestrian.

Decisions like these are particularly important in the City of London, which has the greatest population fluctuation of any city in the world – a square mile with a mere 9,000 permanent residents but more than 300,000 migrant workers travelling in and out every weekday. The City has a far larger proportion than most cities of pedestrians arriving by public transport and then walking to their offices, and that is no accident – City planners design and maintain the Square Mile to favour the pedestrian because it is the only sustainable way to move such huge numbers of people efficiently. The result is that the main mode of transport in the City is on two feet, as seen here crossing London Bridge.

CROWD CONTROL

Not all flocks of pedestrians are commuters; outside the rush hour, sporting events are among the occasions when adults flock on foot in the greatest numbers. Because of the tribal, confrontational nature of many sporting events, different rules apply to managing or controlling the crowds. Unlike flocks of commuters, which are essentially large groups of individuals, crowds of football fans are more unified, share a common purpose, and exhibit a group psychology which makes them much more irascible and much quicker to lose control. The methods police have evolved for managing such crowds can be seen most clearly from above, by looking down on fans arriving for and leaving one of Britain's highest-profile football matches: Rangers v Celtic.

The two teams – and their supporters – are fiercely competitive, and for the police supervising the match this is one of the most complex crowd control operations they ever perform. Their task is to move 60,000 fans in and out of Ibrox stadium in Glasgow while keeping the two sets of supporters entirely separate from each other. On the ground, crowd control may seem chaotic and disorganised but from above it becomes obvious that the police are dealing in a very organised way with the vast and rather touchy snake winding its way through the streets of Glasgow.

This being an annual fixture, the police have had plenty of experience in the best way of managing the crowd, which they do by having two cordons of officers stretching to two separate railway stations, one used by each set of fans. The two sets of supporters are then channelled along pre-planned routes which have been laid out with 'release valves' every few hundred yards – routes down which police can guide people to dissipate the crowd if something goes wrong. Thanks to low-profile, non-confrontational policing, the release valves are rarely needed but, just in case, there are twenty van-loads of reserve police standing by to head off any fans who break through the cordon.

From above it is very clear that adult pedestrians flock in a very different way from the children who pour out of the school gates at the end of the day. In little over a quarter of an hour, every afternoon, over eight million children leave Britain's schools, and for the next hour, the nation's streets are filled with youngsters as they make their way home. Researchers have been studying the difference between children and adult movement patterns by handing GPS trackers to children and plotting their movements to chart what their 'life signatures' look like. Adults, particularly commuters, move in a linear, determined way; their life signatures are purposeful straight lines, whereas children are fundamentally playful and have more random, haphazard life signatures. Where adults move directly from point to point at a fairly consistent speed, children meander and explore and move at different speeds; they stop and chat, dawdle and run. But that pattern of behaviour is changing. More and more children's life signatures are becoming angular, direct and regimented like those of commuting adults – and these are children who are driven to and from school.

GLASTONBURY

Glastonbury is the world's largest performing arts festival. First held in 1970 with an attendance of 1,500, it has grown to be the pre-eminent music festival. Now, with occasional exceptions, it sees an annual migration of more than 150,000 people to Somerset where they create a tented city covering more than 900 acres of farmland. This temporary city has facilities including 3,225 toilets, thousands of food and market stalls, a bank, cash machines, payphones, medical centre, its own FM radio station and standpipes supplying more than a million gallons of drinking water on tap during the course of the festival.

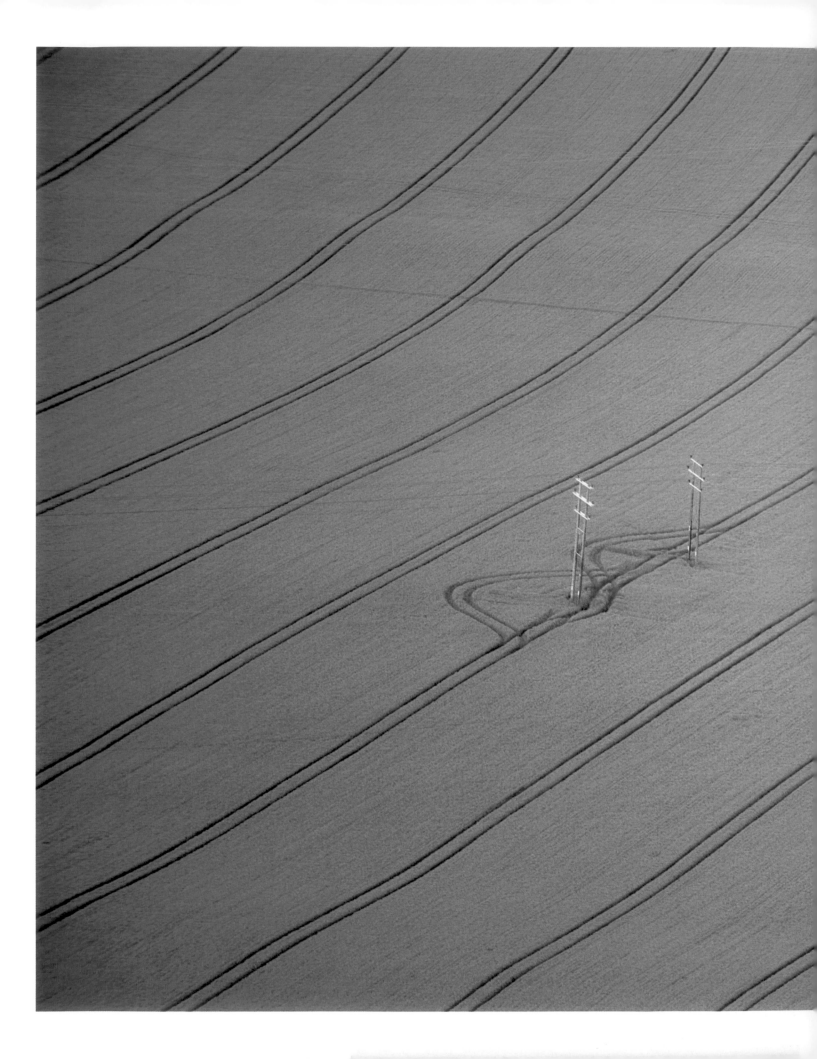

Demand and supply

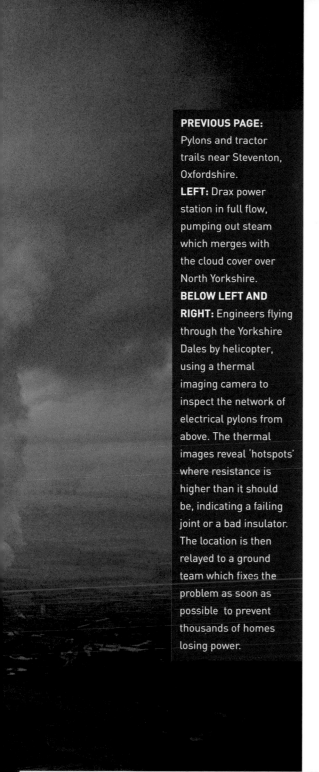

Britain's transport networks are not the only networks that keep the national machine running. To supply the essentials of daily life we also need the vital networks of pipes and cables that keep us warm and watered, the webs of wires and fibre-optics that feed us information and communications, the supply infrastructure that brings us our consumer goods, and the sewers and refuse contractors that take away all our waste. Supplying the nation's needs is a 24/7 cycle of container ships arriving in our ports, fleets of trucks moving goods to our supermarkets and shops, water being pumped from our reservoirs to our homes and from our homes to our sewage works, and electricity being generated in our power stations and supplied to the national grid via nearly 5,000 miles of high-voltage cables. The existence of these networks and infrastructures is often forgotten or taken for granted, but viewed from above, their complexity and efficiency become obvious and spectacular.

Nearly 7 per cent of Britain's total electricity demand is supplied by Drax, the largest coal-fired power station in Britain and the second largest in Europe. Drax, Ferrybridge and Eggborough power stations all stand within 30 miles of each other in the Vale of York, and between them they supply enough electricity to power 7 million homes. But there aren't 7 million homes anywhere near the Vale of York. The reason these power stations are sited here, rather than close to where the power is needed, is that modern power stations are so large they must be built close to supplies of fuel and to the vast amounts of water they need for cooling. It is the latest step in a progression that has seen power generation move from tiny power stations on street corners to the 'cathedrals of power' that supplied entire cities and finally to these modern behemoths sited miles from the centres of demand.

The electricity generated by these stations is transmitted across the national grid at 400,000 and 275,000 volts before being distributed by local supply companies at more manageable voltages. But the national grid is not just a delivery system. It also enables power stations to coordinate their operations to even out fluctuations in generation and consumption, reducing waste by transmitting electricity from where there is the greatest supply, to the areas where there is the greatest demand at any given moment. This is an important function because unlike most commodities, electricity cannot be stored until it is needed – it has to be generated and delivered in the right amounts at the right time.

DUNGENESS

Dungeness is the name of one of the world's largest expanses of shingle. It is also the name of two of the UK's nuclear power stations. Dungeness A, on the right, supplied 446 megawatts to the National Grid from 1965 until 2006 and is currently being decommissioned for conversion into a nuclear waste store. Dungeness B has two 600 megawatt nuclear reactors which began generating in 1983 and is scheduled for closure in 2018. Nuclear power currently accounts for approximately 18 per cent of the UK's electricity, and with the current nuclear power stations all scheduled to close within the next thirty years, the government has announced plans in 2008 to build a new generation of nuclear power stations for the future.

WATER IN WATER OUT

The power stations, pylons and high-voltage cables of the national grid are easy to see from above, but another equally important utility network is largely hidden from view beneath the ground – the UK's water supply and sewerage systems. The average Briton uses 150 litres of water a day, but from above, Britain's reservoirs and sewage works are the only clue to the existence of the hidden network of pipes which deliver that water to our homes and businesses. Every day 19 billion litres of water is drawn from more than 1,500 boreholes, 650 reservoirs and 600 river abstraction points and delivered to the nation's taps via a network of 408,500 kilometres of water mains. And when that water has been used, 11 billion litres are taken away again via another vast network of 373,282 kilometres of sewage pipes to one of the UK's 9,312 sewage works.

Britain's largest sewage works is at Beckton, on the north bank of the Thames in east London. It originated in the 1860s as part of a grand Victorian scheme to improve sanitation in the capital which resulted in the first integrated sewage system in the world. London's waste still runs through the same pipes, thanks to the foresight of engineer Joseph Bazalgette who built his main sewer twice the size required at the time. But unfortunately Bazalgette only built three outflows for the entire system, which

RIGHT: Sedimentation tanks at Britain's – and Europe's – largest sewage works, in Beckton, east London. When London's sewage system was built in the nineteenth century, the sewer at Beckton discharged straight into the river. However, the sewage was washed back into London by the tide, so from 1887 onwards it was treated first and the resulting sludge was taken in special ships and dumped in the North Sea. The Victorian sewage system was a remarkable engineering feat, extending to 1,300 miles of brick-built sewers, most of which are still in use today.

BELOW: Several reservoirs in the Pentland Hills Regional Park store most of the water supply for the nearby city of Edinburgh. Glencorse reservoir, seen here, is known for its breathtaking views and excellent trout fishing. It was created from 1820 to 1824 by building a dam 33.5 metres high and 100 metres wide, and it is linked to Edinburgh by a 9-mile pipeline. Beneath its waters stands a church, which was submerged when the reservoir was created.

means that Beckton has to process the sewage created by the whole of north London: some 3.5 million people, producing enough waste every hour to fill twenty-three Olympic-size swimming pools. But there is a hidden advantage to all that waste – Beckton uses the solid waste as fuel for a sludge-powered generator which produces enough electricity to power over 7,000 homes a year.

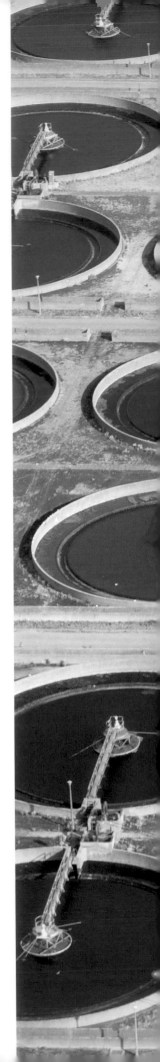

OIL AND GAS

Britain has surprisingly large reserves of oil and natural gas, and primary energy production accounts for 10 per cent of GDP – among the highest of any industrialised nation. Gas was discovered in the North Sea in 1965 and the first major oil discovery was the Forties field, off Aberdeen, in 1970. Britain currently produces some 1.8 million barrels of oil per day and 84.2 billion cubic metres of natural gas per year, making us the world's fifteenth most productive oil nation and sixth most productive for natural gas. These resources are distributed to oil refineries such as this one in the Thames Estuary, and from there to Britain's storage depots and airports, by a network of more than 20,000 miles of pipeline.

JUST IN TIME DELIVERY

Utilities such as electricity, water and gas can be delivered by cable or pipeline but supplying most of our other demands – from daily essentials to imported luxury goods – requires a complex network of ports, depots, warehouses and trucks. The challenge for distributors is to make sure that every supermarket has enough milk and other perishables to meet demand but minimal excess to prevent wastage, and to anticipate massive spikes of consumption caused by everything from increased demand for petrol on bank holidays, to having more flour in the shops on Shrove Tuesday for the nation's pancakes. Christmas is a predictably busy time, with the total number of deliveries of all goods almost doubling, but there are other unpredictable events that distributors need to cope with, such as sudden cold spells leading to increased demand for soup, or sudden hot spells leading to increased demand for drinks, barbecues and garden furniture.

Delivering the right amount of goods at the right time has become a multi-million pound industry which uses computers to calculate everything from minute-by-minute delivery times to the most fuel-efficient speed for trucks to travel on the nation's roads (56-58 mph). Money is lost every time a traffic jam causes a truck to miss its half-hour delivery slot, every time goods are delayed at the port or the warehouse, and every time a retailer's shelves are either too full to too empty – and all of these

things have a knock-on effect on subsequent deliveries which can seriously disrupt the supply chain. Getting all these things right is called 'just in time delivery', and whilst it means consumers usually get what they want when they want it, it also means the system is always on the brink of chaos.

The need for such meticulous organisation becomes obvious in the light of the vast amount of goods arriving at Britain's ports. Approximately 95 per cent of all goods consumed or produced in the UK arrives or leaves by sea, and the UK's fifty-two major ports handle nearly 600 million tons of goods per year. Nearly five million

containers a year arrive at ports such as Felixstowe, Southampton and Tilbury from China and the Far East in specially designed ships which can carry thousands of containers each. That number of containers means that Britain's ports are hugely congested, so one of the UK's biggest distribution companies has pioneered the idea of an inland container port to ease congestion. In 1998 a consortium bought 1,100 acres of the former RAF airfield at Alconbury, Cambridgeshire. Part of the site is already in use as a freight distribution centre, and there are plans to further develop the site with offices, warehouses, retail outlets and 10,000 homes.

LEFT AND ABOVE: The runways of the former RAF airfield at Alconbury are being transformed into an 'inland container port' with the capacity to store thousands of containers of goods before they are distributed around the country. Alconbury was established as an RAF airfield in 1938 and used by the US Air Force from 1942 to 1995. Most of the site was sold in 1998 and is currently being redeveloped as a national freight distribution centre.

Up to 2,500 containers can be moved immediately from Felixstowe, Britain's biggest container port, to the 'inland port' at Alconbury, whose vast aprons and runways of flat concrete are ideal for moving and storing containers. From Alconbury the goods are transported to regional distribution centres around the country and then onwards via local supply chains into Britain's temples of commerce – our shops, supermarkets and out-of-town retail parks.

ISLE OF SHEPPEY

Sheppey is a small island off the Kent coast whose main port, Sheerness, is one of Britain's largest car-handling terminals. With 260 acres of car compounds, Sheerness handles some 400,000 imported cars each year, including cars made by Peugeot, Citroen, VW, Audi, SEAT, Skoda, Subaru, Daihatsu, Porsche and Honda. Sheerness originated as a sixteenth-century fort built by Henry VIII to protect the River Medway from invasion. In 1667 the fort failed to prevent the Dutch sailing up the Medway and destroying the pride of the English fleet, so two years later, Samuel Pepys, diarist and Secretary to the Admiralty, helped establish a naval dockyard there. The closure of the dockyard in 1960 devastated Sheppey's economy, but cheap land and good road and rail connections meant that the dockyard was successfully redeveloped as a commercial port. As the Port of Sheerness it is now thriving as a major importer of fresh produce, forest products and foreign cars.

A NATION OF SHOPPERS

It was Napoleon who first observed that England is a nation of shopkeepers, and from the air it seems that he was right – shopping is part of the national psyche, not just of England but the whole of Britain. But the nature of shopkeeping has changed since Napoleon's time. The corner shop and the high street are no longer the main providers – instead, millions of Britons a day jump in their cars and drive to the supermarket or one of the vast new temples of commerce and consumption, the out-of-town shopping centre. Over the last twenty-five years the amount of space given over to shops up and down the UK has quadrupled, and in an average day we spend more than £350 million on credit cards and more than £600 million on debit cards – that's nearly 1 billion pounds a day without even taking cash transactions into account.

On top of the billion pounds a day we spend on plastic, we also use vast amounts of cash. A single security van might carry up to £10 million in cash, and in a single day, fleets of vans ferry nearly £1.4 billion around the country in notes and coins. At one time people would be paid in cash or travel to their bank to withdraw what they needed, but even withdrawing cash has now become a matter of convenience and the subject of another hidden supply network.

On 27 June 1967, actor Reg Varney opened the world's first cash machine at Barclays Bank in Enfield, north London. Thus Barclays started a trend which now sees some 61,000 cash machines across the country dispensing nearly 70 per cent of the cash used in the UK. The maximum withdrawal at the first cashpoint was £10 but forty years later the average withdrawal was £65.34 and cash machine users were making more than 2.75 billion withdrawals per year – an average of more than eighty-seven withdrawals every second of every day.

LEFT AND ABOVE: Bluewater Shopping Centre near Greenhithe, Kent. This massive shopping centre has 155,700 square metres of retail floor space, making it Britain's second biggest shopping centre after the MetroCentre in Gateshead, Tyne & Wear, and the fourth biggest in Europe. Opened in 1999, Bluewater occupies 240 acres of a disused chalk quarry and has 333 shops, more than forty food and drink outlets, a twelve-screen cinema and a climbing wall. It has parking for 13,000 cars and 100 coaches, and serves some 27 million people per year, or nearly 75,000 every day.

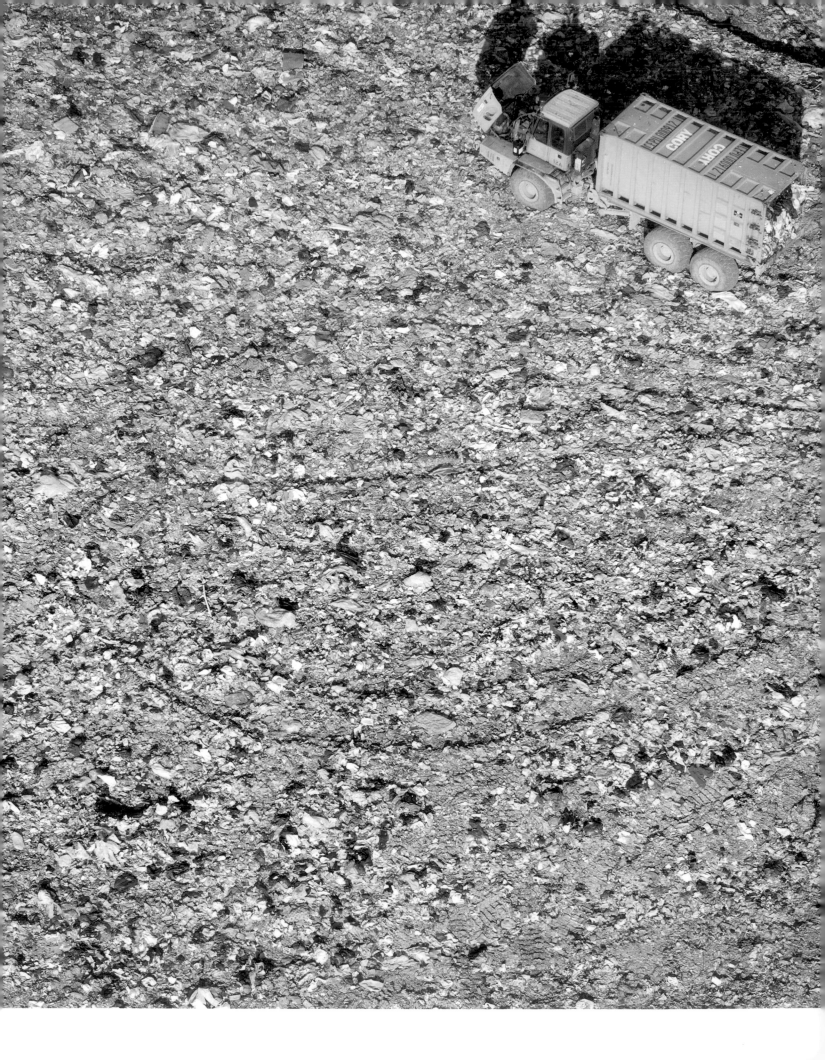

WASTELANDS

Inevitably the more we consume the more we throw away, and the logistics of waste disposal are almost as complicated as the logistics of supplying goods in the first place. There are more than 100,000 waste disposal vehicles spread throughout the UK, and every day they pick up almost 50,000 tons of rubbish and drive it to incinerators or to landfill sites such as Britain's largest landfill, Mucking Marshes in Essex. Already 109 square miles of the UK – an area the size of Manchester – has been filled with our rubbish and we're still adding 16.9 million tons a year to landfill despite hundreds of thousands of tons of waste actually leaving the country.

Nearly 70 per cent of our recyclable plastic is exported to China, which has a huge demand for waste plastic as a raw material for making new products. And under an EU directive, retailers are now obliged to take back redundant white goods such as fridges, freezers and washing machines when customers buy new ones. The old machines are collected by the same lorries and distribution companies

LEFT AND BELOW: Trucks like mechanised dinosaurs are constantly adding to the millions of tons of rubbish at Mucking Marshes, which is Britain's largest landfill site and one of the largest in Europe. The 300 hectare site, a former gravel quarry near the Essex village of Mucking, handles about a fifth of London's waste. The rubbish arrives in yellow containers that travel more than 30 miles down the Thames on barges – saving a reported 65,000 journeys by HGV – before being loaded onto the trucks at a wharf on the edge of the site. The landscape around Mucking is totally flat, and the hill up which the trucks are climbing in the picture below is entirely made up of rubbish. In 2007, operators Cory Environmental were given permission to use the site until 2010, during which time they expect to landfill an extra 1.2 million tons of waste and add 3 metres to the height of the mound, after which the plan is to grass it over and turn it into a community park.

that deliver new machines to the shops, crushed in recycling centres, and then packed into empty containers and shipped back to China. There, the waste materials are used for making new machines as part of an endless cycle of consumption and disposal.

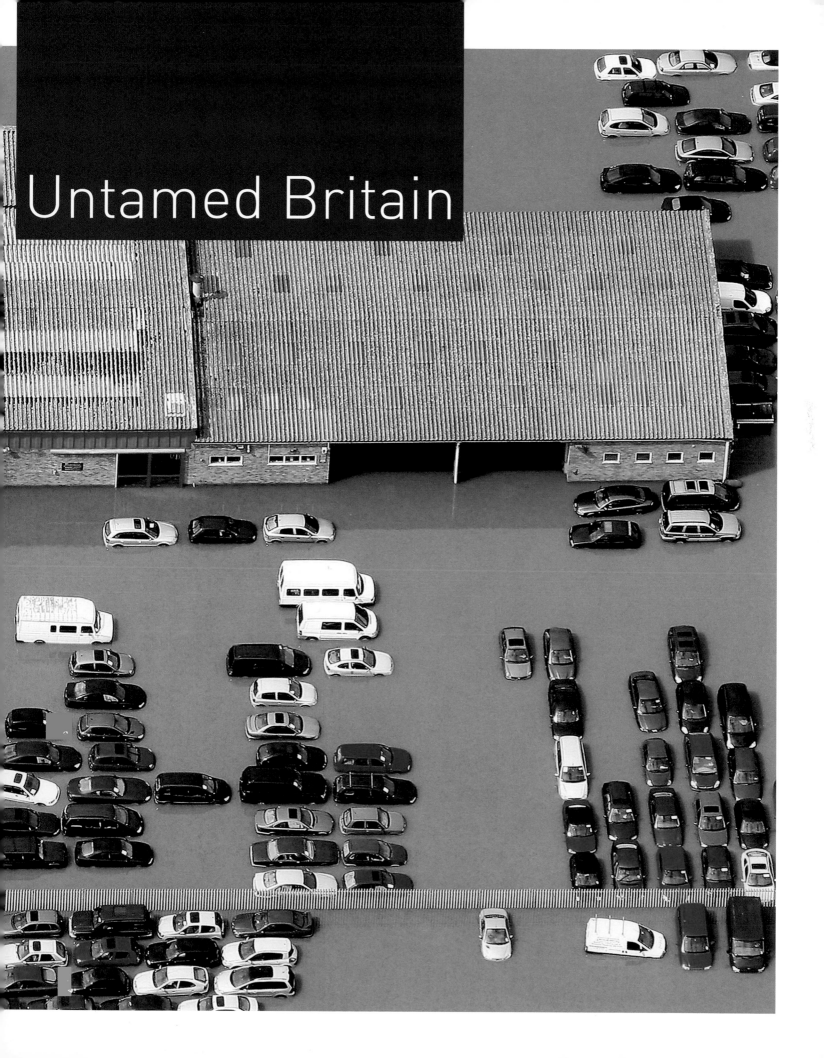

Untamed Britain

The weather is a national obsession for Britons. We are notorious for using it as a conversational gambit and for always complaining that it's too hot or too cold or too changeable. But there is a good reason for that – because of Britain's geographical position our weather *is* exceptionally changeable, as becomes clear when our weather systems are seen from above.

Forecasters use satellite images to track weather systems as they approach the UK. But even with the latest technology, forecasting is a huge challenge because Britain lies at the confluence of up to six weather systems, with winds from the Atlantic, Europe, the Arctic, and the Sahara bringing abrupt, cold snaps or heatwaves, snowstorms or floods. This means that although the Met Office uses cutting-edge technology, weather forecasting remains as much an art as a science, and it takes years of experience before a forecaster can look at a series of satellite images and have any real sense of what type of weather might hit the country next.

One of the things that drives Britain's weather systems is cloud formation, and one of the ways in which clouds form is through convection, which occurs when the sun heats up the earth or the sea causing warm, damp air to rise in currents known as thermals. Thermals are invisible but their presence becomes apparent when we see birds or hang-gliders defying gravity by rising in graceful spirals as they ride the updraughts, some of which are so powerful they can lift a hang-glider more than 3,050 metres. But a thermal is not just a column of air – it also contains gallons of evaporating water. One acre of a cereal crop can evaporate up to 4,000 gallons of moisture in a single day, which slowly cools until, at a certain altitude, it condenses into clouds.

HERE COMES THE RAIN AGAIN

LEFT AND BELOW:
Widespread flooding during July 2007 devastated large areas of Britain, including Gloucestershire and Warwickshire where the Rivers Severn and Avon burst their banks. Being raised above the level of the surrounding fields, this road near Tewkesbury, Gloucestershire, narrowly escaped the flooding but the caravan park just outside Tiddington, near Stratford-upon-Avon, was not so lucky.

The clouds that move in from the Atlantic or form over Britain's land mass not only shape our weather, they also shape the nation's landscape. Of all the natural forces unleashed on Britain, the rain has the most powerful cumulative effect – 2.5 mm of rain falling on 1 acre of land weighs 113 tons, and over millenia an incredible weight of water has carved valleys through Britain's hills, filled the nation's lakes, and fed the meandering curves of its great rivers as they wind their way to the sea. Many of Britain's greatest towns and cities have grown up along these rivers but the rain can be cruel as well as kind, and when hard rain really starts falling, living by a river is not always the best place to be.

The rain requires an entire national infrastructure to manage and contain it, and that infrastructure is often tested to its limits and sometimes beyond. In 2007 Britain experienced the wettest May to July period in 251 years, since rainfall records began in 1766. The resulting deluge overwhelmed the banks of rivers up and down the UK, causing floods which killed fourteen people, closed six motorways, and devastated more than 55,000 homes and businesses at an estimated cost of £4 billion. Flooding is nothing new but the scale of the 2007 floods was enormous and, significantly, the disaster differed from other severe floods in that a much higher proportion of the floodwater than normal came from surface water rather than

rivers. According to the official Environment Agency report, two-thirds of the properties flooded were affected because drains and sewers were overwhelmed rather than by rivers bursting their banks.

The reason for this unusual flood feature is Britain's relentless building programme. In the past much of the floodwater would have soaked into the land or drained away through streams and rivers, but we are laying down thousands of acres of concrete and tarmac in the form of new roads, housing developments, retail parks and shopping centres, and in the process altering the water tables and rain-water flows that have

developed over millennia. Even seemingly innocuous changes have a cumulative effect – for instance, some 66 per cent of London's front gardens have been paved in the last twenty years; an area equivalent to twenty-two Hyde Parks. This means that heavy rainfall is no longer absorbed by the ground or fed naturally into the rivers but runs away into gutters, drains and sewers which are often overwhelmed, or flows through emergency drains directly into rivers which aren't able to cope with the massive extra flow. The result, as Britain discovered in 2007, can be disastrous.

ABOVE: The futuristic Thames Flood Barrier, which was built to protect London from flooding when high tides coincide with storm surges from the North Sea. London is no stranger to catastrophic flooding: the earliest account, dated 1099, records that 'the sea flood sprang up to such a height and did so much harm as no man remembered that it ever did before,' and in 1633 diarist Samuel Pepys wrote that 'there was last night the greatest tide that was ever remembered in England to have been in this river, all Whitehall being drowned.' The idea of a flood barrier was floated as long ago as the 1850s but it did not become a reality until more than a hundred years later. Built between 1975 and 1984, this is the world's second-largest moveable flood barrier, comprising four large and six small retractable gates with a total span of 523 metres. The curved gates lie in concrete sills on the riverbed and in the event of a flood warning they are rotated through 90°, rising up and sealing off the channels between the gleaming steel machine housings. The barrier has been raised more than 100 times in earnest and every time so far it has stopped the tide – small wonder that at the opening ceremony the Queen called it 'the Eighth Wonder of the World'. However, there are fears that as sea levels continue to rise and south-east England continues to sink, an even bigger barrier will have to be built further downstream.

LEFT: Gloucester completely surrounded by floodwater on 24 July 2007. As a result of the flooding more than a third of a million people across Gloucestershire were left without running water, tens of thousands suffered power cuts and thousands were forced to flee their homes.

STAYING DRY

Ironically, for a country where people complain that it rains frequently and where flooding is an increasing problem, Britain is much closer to drought than many people realise. The reservoirs and groundwater supplies of England and Wales contain less than 1,500 cubic metres of water per person per year, which is less than half the reserves per head of Italy or Spain. The problem is even worse in south-east England, where the high density of population means that water reserves per head are only one-fifth of the national average.

It is not just long, hot summers that deplete water reserves; dry winters are an even greater problem, because it is winter rainfall that consolidates the groundwater which provides about 30 per cent of our water supplies. And the effects of drought are not confined to humans having to put up with occasional hosepipe bans and, even more rarely, standpipes in the street. During a drought, vast areas of the landscape become susceptible to fire, and wildlife that rely on ponds or streams for feeding or breeding are also affected.

Parts of Britain have suffered drought in each of the last four decades. In 1976 reservoirs ran dry as early as May, and at the end of August a brief rain shower made headline news. Hosepipe bans were strictly enforced and as the summer wore on, hundreds of thousands of households in Wales, western England and Yorkshire had their water cut off and had to use standpipes for some or all of each day. Industrial water supplies were rationed, forcing several companies to impose a short working week, and forest fires raged across the south of England destroying hundreds of acres of the New Forest and other woodland. The government was so concerned it even went so far as to appoint a Minister for Drought.

The 1980s and 1990s each saw less acute but longer-lasting droughts as year on year, light

winter rain failed to replenish groundwater, and the same occurred again from 2003-2006. In March 2006 *National Geographic* magazine reported that parts of England were desperately short of water following the driest sixteen-month period in more than seventy years, and quoted the Environment Agency's statement that there was less water available per head in southern England than in Sudan. In April, for the first time in fifteen years, Thames Water imposed a ban on hosepipes and sprinklers, and by July, eight water companies had imposed hosepipe bans on 13 million people across south-east England. Yet within a year Britain was experiencing the wettest summer since records began, and vast swathes of the country lay underwater after unprecedented flooding.

THE POWER OF THE WIND

LEFT: Scores of trees uprooted at a country house in Kent during the Great Storm of 1987. Fifteen million trees were destroyed including – according to legend – six of the seven oaks after which the Kent town of Sevenoaks was named. In fact the six lost oaks had been planted in 1902 as part of a civic tradition. The town is named after a much earlier seven oaks and has been known as such since at least the thirteenth century.
RIGHT: Harnessing the power of the wind for leisure – kite surfing at Exmouth, Devon. This sport developed during the 1990s and there are now more than 200,000 kite surfers worldwide. The power of the wind can propel surfers at speeds of more than 40 knots.
FAR RIGHT: Harnessing the power of the wind for electricity – a maintenance platform alongside one of the thirty turbines at Scroby Sands Wind Farm, near Great Yarmouth. The hollow steel mast of each turbine rises 68 metres above mean sea level and has three 40-metre blades attached, generating up to 2 megawatts. At full capacity the farm generates enough electricity to power 30-40,000 homes.

Every day billions of cubic metres of air sweep across the British Isles as they move from areas of high pressure to areas of low pressure. These winds bring with them frequent changes in the weather and, remarkably, they often spiral into tornadoes – Britain sees up to fifty tornadoes per year, a higher frequency per square mile than anywhere else in the world. Thankfully they are far smaller than their US cousins, but Britain's 'tornado alley' stretches across the Midlands, central southern England, the South-east and East Anglia.

Although local wind speeds and directions vary greatly, they tend to blow primarily from one direction. This is known as the prevailing wind, and it has affected everything from the siting and alignment of wind farms to the evolution of Britain's cities. Every town and city is different but from above there is a discernible pattern to urban development, with an 'old town' at the centre, surrounded by waves of expansion which typically see the well-to-do areas to the west and the industrial and working class areas to the east. The reason this arrangement is so common is that Britain's prevailing winds are westerly (ie, they blow from west to east).

The stench of medieval towns, and the industrial smoke and grime of later ones, would therefore be carried primarily in one direction – to the east.

Britain is lucky that the wind rarely wreaks such widespread destruction as the 'Great Storm of 1987' that hit northern France and southern England on the night of 15-16 October that year. On the evening of 15 October, BBC weatherman Michael Fish infamously laughed off a viewer's suggestion that there might be a hurricane imminent. Hours later winds were gusting up to 100 mph, and overnight the storm killed twenty-two people (four of them in France) and uprooted 15 million trees, leaving a trail of destruction from Cornwall to East Anglia. The following day a quarter of a million homes were without power, Gatwick Airport was temporarily closed and no mainline trains were running south of the Midlands. The Met Office admitted that forecasts 'left much to be desired' but technically Michael Fish was right – by definition a hurricane is a tropical storm and this one did not develop in the tropics so despite the hurricane force winds it was not, officially, a hurricane.

BLACK LAW WIND FARM

It is particularly apt that Black Law, the UK's most powerful wind farm, was built on the site of an old open-cast coal-mine. This huge wind farm in Lanarkshire was opened in 2006 with forty-two 2.3 megawatt turbines. Twelve more have since been added, giving Black Law the capacity to power some 70,000 homes and thus saving an estimated 200,000 tons of carbon dioxide emissions every year. During construction, the land around the turbines was restored to create 14 square kilometres of shallow wetlands and 24 kilometres of public footpaths.

THE POWER OF THE WAVES

It is said that every day, on average, waves collide with the British coastline with the cumulative force of several atomic bombs. At present this vast amount of energy is largely wasted but since the oil crisis of the 1970s, scientists have been investigating ways of harnessing the power of the waves to generate electricity. The world's first commercial wave farm is already operating in Portugal, and during 2007 plans were announced for wave farms off the coasts of California, Cornwall and Orkney. Advocates of renewable energy are not the only fans of big waves – they are also a boon for the thousands of British surfers who flock to the coast each summer – but for many others, the waves are a destructive nuisance, wreaking havoc on coastal transport systems and endangering coastal villages through cliff erosion.

LEFT: Fish on the line... Waves batter a passenger train as it passes along the coastal railway line at Dawlish in Devon, en route from Newton Abbot to Exeter. On the same October evening, another train was stuck on the line as the high tides and severe gales created ferocious waves around the entire south-west coast.

BELOW: Wooden coastal defences at Happisburgh, Norfolk. These timber defences were built in 1959 but after twenty years of battering by the wind and waves they began failing in the 1980s, allowing the sea to erode the cliffs ever more rapidly. Various proposals were put forward for new sea defences but while they were under consideration the sea encroached so far and so fast that the proposals became unworkable. Local residents continue to campaign for better sea defences but a government quango recently recommended allowing the sea to breach the coast, flooding an area of some 25 square miles. The result would be a new bay which would drown 1.2 per cent of Norfolk including several historic windmills, hundreds of acres of farmland and six villages, with some 600 homes and five medieval churches.

HAPPISBURGH

The waves are eroding the Norfolk coastline at a rate of tens of metres per decade and the village of Happisburgh is fast disappearing into the sea (see previous page). Only twelve years ago the terraced houses at the centre of this picture were separated from the cliff edge by long gardens, their own garages, a road and another row of houses (see page 110) – now they are in danger of collapsing into the sea at every storm tide as the waves eat further and further inland.

ORFORD NESS

While parts of the British coastline are being eroded at
an alarming rate, the power of the waves is altering other
parts by the opposite process: accretion. Orford Ness is a
spit of shingle deposits stretching some 10 miles along the
Suffolk coast from Aldeburgh to North Weir Point, cutting
off direct access from Orford to the sea. For hundreds of
years the shingle has been carried by the sea from further
north and deposited here through a process called
longshore drift, creating the largest vegetated shingle
spit in Europe. The Ness served as a military test site
from 1913 until the end of the Cold War, and under its
current status as a National Nature Reserve it is now
home to a number of rare species in varied habitats
including shingle, saltmarsh, mudflats, sandflats,
grassland and brackish lagoons. The Ness is separated
from the mainland by the River Alde.

The future

Viewing Britain from above reveals our nation in an entirely new light. It allows us to see how the natural landscape has evolved over thousands, and even millions, of years, and how networks and infrastructures have developed over time. But what of the future? Current patterns can also provide us with clues to what Britain might look like in years to come.

Aerial views of existing 'new towns' hint at the direction urban planning might take; satellite views of fields show how our use of land for agriculture is evolving; and computer-generated models show how our city skylines might change over the next fifty years. The immediate future is easier to predict. Thanks to architects' visualisations, we already have a good idea of how east London, for example, is likely to change as a result of the 2012 Olympics.

The centrepiece of the Olympic Park will be an 80,000-seat stadium which will host the Opening and Closing Ceremonies and the athletics events. In a revolutionary departure for stadium construction, 55,000 seats and the upper part of the stadium will be demountable. After the Games the seats will be removed, leaving a permanent 25,000-seat arena for sports, community and educational uses. The field of play and the permanent seating will be incorporated in a sunken bowl built into the ground, with the demountable steel superstructure rising above it. The superstructure will be protected by a 28-metre-wide cable-supported roof, and the entire stadium will be wrapped in a 20-metre high fabric 'curtain' depicting Olympic heroes from history.

PREVIOUS PAGE: Fuel of the future? Oilseed Rape could dominate the countryside.
TOP: Visualisation of the London 2012 Olympic Stadium in the 2008 London cityscape. The stadium will stand between two branches of the River Lea (aka Lee), and access will be via footbridges.
BOTTOM: Visualisation of the London 2012 Olympic Aquatics Centre, designed by award-winning architect Zaha Hadid. Hadid said her inspiration for the distinctive sweeping roof was 'the fluid geometry of water in motion, creating spaces and a surrounding environment in sympathy with the river landscape'. The Aquatics Centre will host the swimming, diving and synchronised swimming events, as well as the water polo finals and parts of the modern pentathlon. The plan is that after the Games 15,000 temporary seats – housed in temporary structures attached to the sides of the building – will be removed, leaving east London with a 2,500-seat swimming and diving venue.
LEFT: Visualisation of the London 2012 Olympic park.

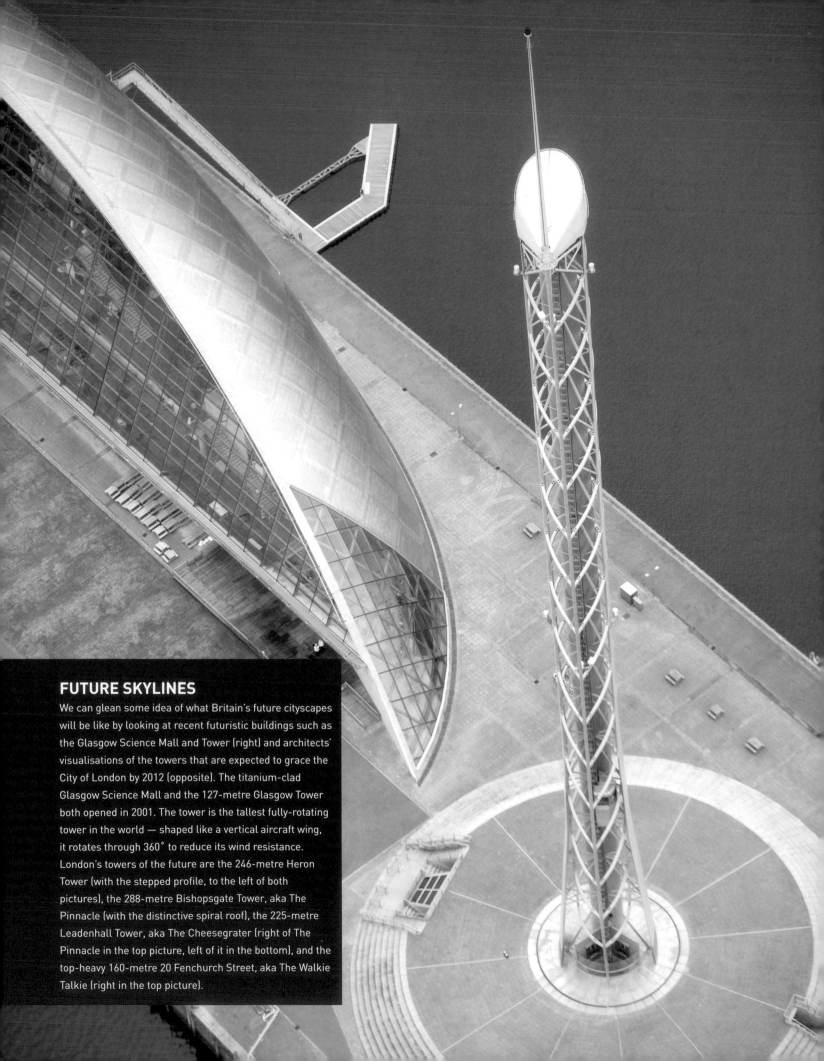

FUTURE SKYLINES

We can glean some idea of what Britain's future cityscapes will be like by looking at recent futuristic buildings such as the Glasgow Science Mall and Tower (right) and architects' visualisations of the towers that are expected to grace the City of London by 2012 (opposite). The titanium-clad Glasgow Science Mall and the 127-metre Glasgow Tower both opened in 2001. The tower is the tallest fully-rotating tower in the world — shaped like a vertical aircraft wing, it rotates through 360° to reduce its wind resistance. London's towers of the future are the 246-metre Heron Tower (with the stepped profile, to the left of both pictures), the 288-metre Bishopsgate Tower, aka The Pinnacle (with the distinctive spiral roof), the 225-metre Leadenhall Tower, aka The Cheesegrater (right of The Pinnacle in the top picture, left of it in the bottom), and the top-heavy 160-metre 20 Fenchurch Street, aka The Walkie Talkie (right in the top picture).

DEVELOPING THE GREEN BELT

As the population increases and Britain becomes more crowded, increasing amounts of farmland may be taken up with 'new towns' like Bar Hill, which was built in the 1960s to ease housing shortages in Cambridgeshire. The development was built from scratch on 350 acres of farmland as a self-contained residential and commercial village of 4,000 people. The road layout included no straight lines and each home was designed and placed to give it a more rural feel. Traffic was to be largely restricted to the perimeter road and a network of footpaths linked all the houses to the shopping precinct.

CAMBOURNE NEW TOWN

Cambourne in Cambridgeshire is another example of how increasing amounts of British farmland might look in the future. Work began in 1998 with planning permission for 3,300 homes and the first phase is expected to be complete by 2010, although there are already proposals for 700 more homes. Because it is built on former farmland there is nothing to restrict developers. Cambourne even has a carefully landscaped cemetery, but the development is so new that as yet no-one is buried in it.

FUTURE TRANSPORT

ABOVE: A familiar sight in pre-war Britain, trams are returning to the streets of an increasing number of British cities. Nottingham Express Transit (pictured) opened its first line in 2004 and has proved so successful that proposals are underway to build a second line, extending the network to 19 miles. When the second line opens in 2013, passenger numbers are projected to double to 20 million journeys per year, or nearly 55,000 per day.

RIGHT: The Cambridgeshire Guided Busway (CGB) under construction through open fields near Cambridge. A guided bus is a cross between a bus and a tram, being a road-going vehicle that is guided along some or all of its route on a dedicated guideway which excludes other traffic. Guided busways are likely to become increasingly common in the near future – eight British cities already have at least some short sections of guideway and such routes are planned for eleven more cities. The route of the CBG will utilise some 17 miles of newly-built guideway, part of which will follow the route of the disused Ely & St Ives Railway, as well as making part of the journey unguided on public roads. Construction began in 2007 and is scheduled for completion in 2009, when the CBG will be the world's longest guided busway. It is expected to carry more than 11,000 passengers per day, helping to reduce congestion on the A14.

ASPARAGUS PICKERS

Asparagus pickers in Barford, Warwickshire. The British asparagus season runs from mid-April until 21 June and Britons eat a phenomenal amount of it – some 2,000 tons of home-grown asparagus per year (more than 50 million spears). Before the Second World War farmworkers were a common sight in Britain's fields but with the rapid mechanisation that followed the war they became increasingly rare. But asparagus has to be picked by hand and if concerns about food miles increase and more asparagus is grown in the UK we are likely to see ever more workers in our fields.

OILSEED RAPE

At one time Britain's fields were green, golden or brown depending on the season, but since the Second World War an increasing number are bright yellow with oilseed rape, as vividly illustrated in this satellite image of Essex and Suffolk. The trend is set to continue as the use of oilseed rape widens to include bio-fuels. Production is increasing rapidly – in 1965 the world produced just over 5 million tons, and forty years later, in 2005, that had increased nine-fold to more than 45 million tons. Britain is currently the sixth largest producer at nearly 2 million tons per year.

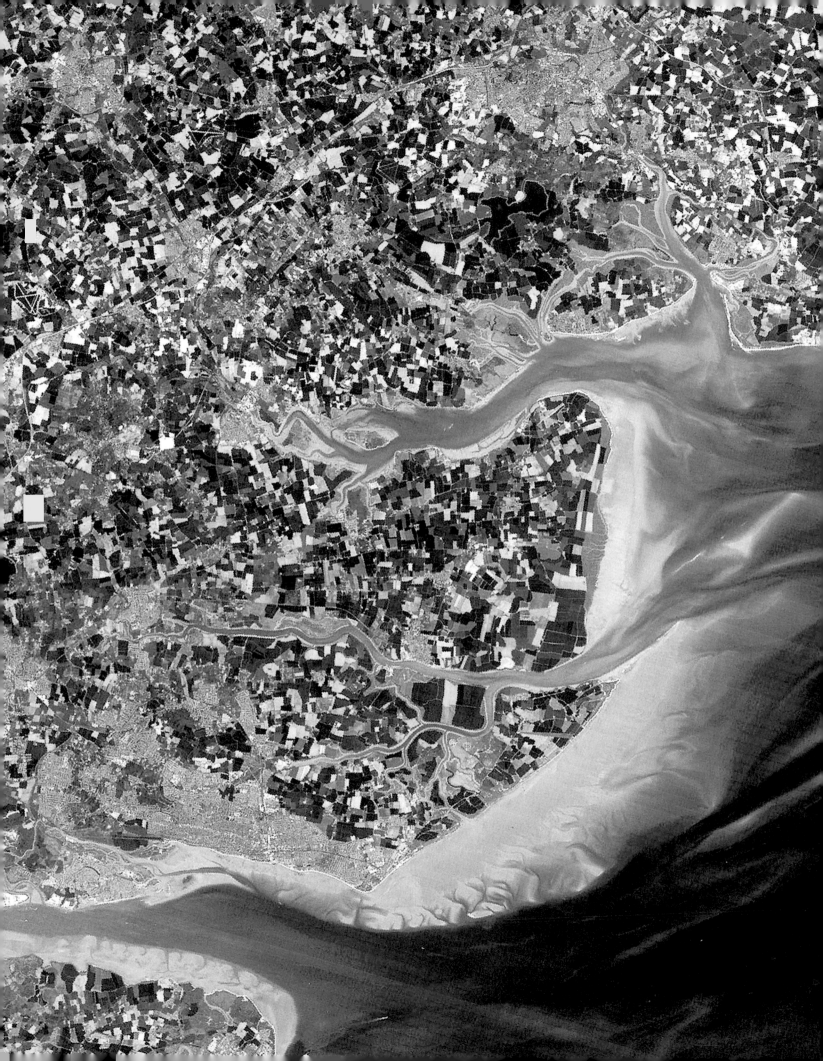

HOTHOUSES

As Britons become more conscious of their impact on the environment, the issue of 'food miles' – the amount of energy used up in transporting non-seasonal foods from hot climates to our supermarket shelves – is having an increasing effect on our agriculture. Consumers expect out-of-season produce but they want it home-grown, which means that farmers are increasingly looking at ways to extend the season of native crops, and to grow non-native crops, using poly tunnels, greenhouses and hothouses. Blue fields of hothouses, like this one in North Kent, are likely to become an increasingly common sight.

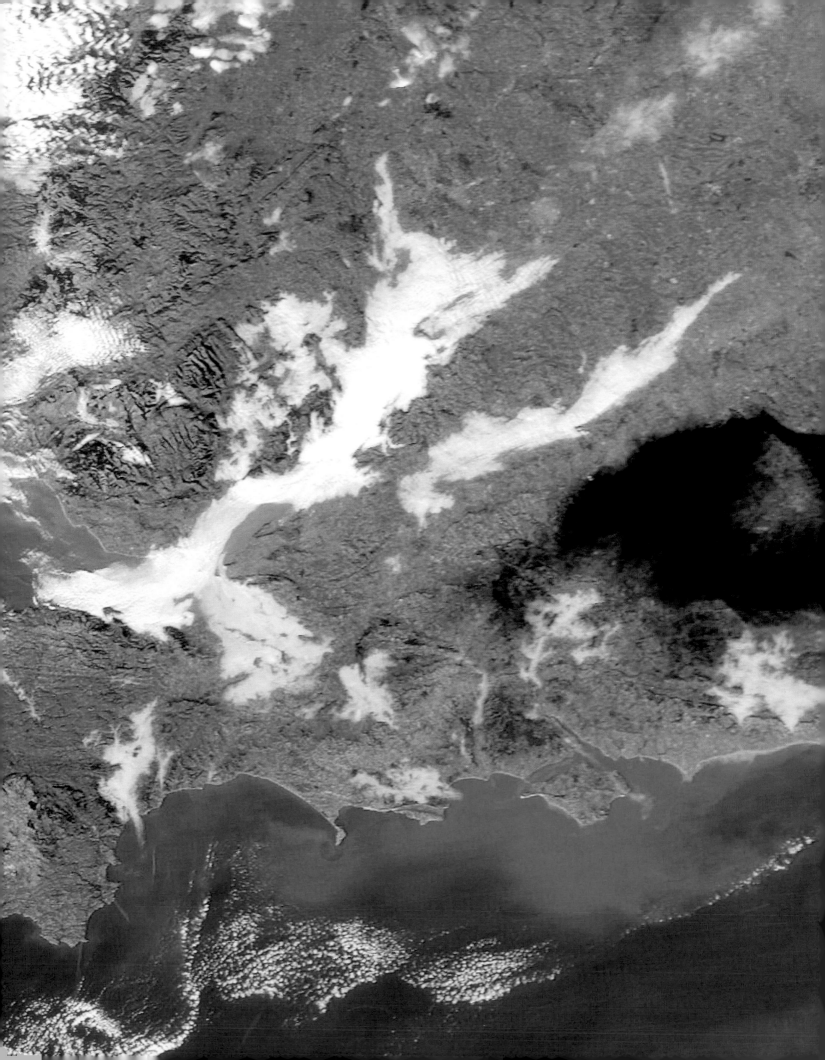

FUTURE HAZARDS

As Britain becomes more crowded it is not necessarily the most obvious things – such as military installations and nuclear power stations – that will present the greatest public hazards. Industrial sites such as chemical works, paint factories and oil depots are all potentially hazardous, as became all too clear in December 2005 after an explosion and fire at the Hertfordshire Oil Storage Terminal, better known as the Buncefield Depot. The initial explosion was heard more than 100 miles away and measured 2.4 on the Richter scale, while fire chiefs said the blaze, which burned for fifty-nine hours, was the largest in peacetime Europe. The smoke plume, seen in this satellite image, rose to an estimated 3,350 metres.

LEFT: Balanced precariously on a crane above the M6/M5 motorway junction, director Cassian Harrison and director of photography, Lee Pulbrook, wait for phantom traffic jams to appear out of nowhere.

RIGHT: The crew turn Miner 49ers and pan for gold in Ulster.

LEFT: Andrew Marr discusses the problems of crowd control with Senior Lecturer in social psychology Dr. Clifford Stott as Glasgow Celtic fans spill out of the Ibrox stadium onto the streets of Glasgow after an 'Old Firm' game against Rangers.

ABOVE: Director Nic Young gazes out over the capital city from the roof of New London Bridge House and contemplates the vast changes that have shaped the city. The element was included in the BBC2 film, *The City Transformed*.

ABOVE AND LEFT: Adding further weight to the theory that he is the thinking woman's John Noakes, Andrew Marr prepares to be bundled out of a plane at 12,000 feet above Norfolk. Andrew confessed to the *Mail on Sunday*, 'I have a sneaking suspicion that *Britain From Above* is morphing into *What Can We Do To Big Ears Next?*' He describes skydiving as '...nothing like you see in pictures when sky-divers seem to float in the air. You don't float. You plummet, at an astonishing speed. I'm not a Quaver, I'm a projectile. Then there is a great jerk and the parachute opens.'

ABOVE: Locating the presenter in the crowded streets of London from 1,000 feet up is not easy, so on a sunny day outside Liverpool Street station, the production team give aerial director Michael Malric-Smith a visual aid.

THE MAKING OF BRITAIN FROM ABOVE

RIGHT: Andrew Marr's very first day on location with the *Britain From Above* team and he prepares for a stunning flight over the Great Glen of Scotland. Two microlite aircraft were used, one with Andrew on board, the other with vulcanologist Dr. Dougal Jerram talking about the rocks beneath our feet.

BELOW: The production team make the final flight checks on the second microlite aircraft before sending them into the skies and pursuing them with a helicopter. Andrew later referred to his craft as, 'a propeller-driven tricycle with a fabric triangle on top.'

LEFT: Nicola Lloyd, producer of the 'Behind the Scenes' films for the website, captures the action as Andrew Marr is launched on a tandem paraglider to circle the skies with up to sixty hang-gliders above the Welsh borders.

RIGHT: Looking to all the world like a blue grasshopper - Castle Air provided the aerial filming platform and were required to chase an amazing variety of 'aircraft' through the series, from hang-gliders and paragliders, to microlites, biplanes, Cessna light aircraft and an RAF Typhoon.

LEFT: Sound recordist Grant Lawson eavesdrops on the paraglider briefing as Andrew Marr prepares to ride the thermals in one of the most spectacular sequences from the series.

LEFT: Michael Malric-Smith and director of aerial photography Peter Thompson had no problems keeping up with a couple of Tiger Moths during filming, but were 'pushing the envelope' when it came to keeping pace with the RAF's latest strike aircraft.

CASTLE AIR — PETER THOMPSON
CASTLE AIR — MICHAEL MALRIC-SMITH

RIGHT: Series producer Lucy van Beek monitors the cloud speeds over Glastonbury in consultation with the balloon pilots. The windows for flying at Glastonbury were dawn and dusk on Friday, and dawn on Saturday, but the wind didn't ease up long enough to allow a technical recce, let alone a shoot.

ABOVE: Aerial stills photographer Jason Hawkes poses with his long-time collaborator, pilot Ian Evans. Jason's brief took him to St.Austell, Rhondda, Glasgow, Ayr, Sheffield, Manchester, Norfolk, Kent and Glastonbury among many locations. The MoD's Eastern Europe-style village, Copehill, on Salisbury Plain, was the only one that got away.

LEFT: Head of photography, Lee Pulbrook, and sound recordist, Grant Lawson, run through the technical requirements of strapping valuable recording equipment to a whicker basket that is likely to end up in a heavy impact.

ABOVE: The best-laid plans... are frequently rearranged by the weather. No more so than at Glastonbury where, in a makeshift meeting room, the production team try to re-arrange a shoot that has taken three weeks to set up... in an hour. Lucy van Beek scrambles a Tiger Moth biplane from East Anglia, while line producer Rebecca Winch (standing right) tries to convince the aerial director that his stand-down time should coincide precisely with the times that Leonard Cohen and Neil Diamond take to the stage.

RIGHT: Andrew Marr signs off the series from Glastonbury before disappearing with the team to see acts ranging from the Fratellis to Amy Winehouse.

INDEX

Picture Credits

The publisher would like to thank the following for their help in supplying images for the book, in particular Jason Hawkes and Zoe Caldwell at www.jasonhawkes.com. Thanks also to Michael Malric-Smith and Peter Thompson from Castle Air for the HD grabs, Liz Jenkins at the National Monuments Record office (NMR) and Kevin McLaren at the Royal Commission on the Ancient Historical Monuments of Scotland (RCAHMS), plus the Lion TV Assistant Producers.

Code: R=Right, L=Left, T=Top, B=Bottom, C=Centre

Page 208 caption: Bowness-on-Solway, Cumbria

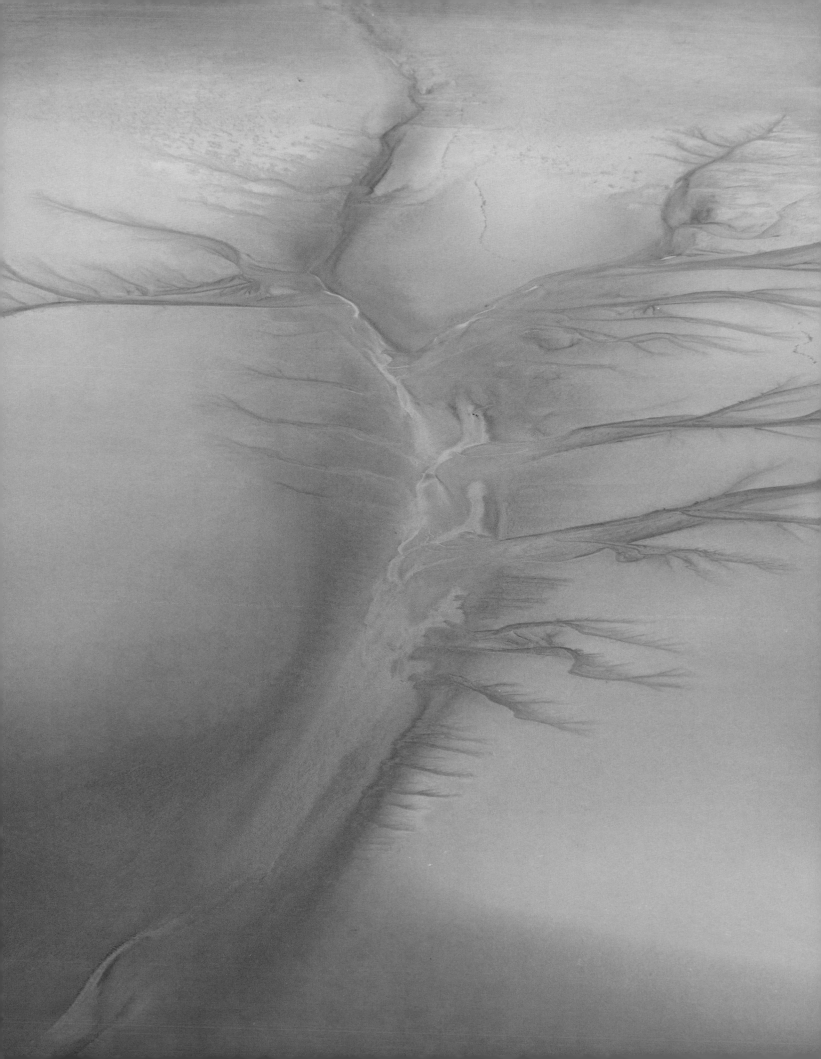